CRM
Concepts & Practices in Hotel and Tourism Operations

CRM
Concepts & Practices in Hotel and Tourism Operations

Bibhuti Bhushan Pradhan
Sasmita Mohanty
Ashish Mohanty

BLACK EAGLE BOOKS
Dublin, USA | Bhubaneswar, India

 Black Eagle Books
USA address:
7464 Wisdom Lane
Dublin, OH 43016

India address:
E/312, Trident Galaxy, Kalinga Nagar,
Bhubaneswar-751003, Odisha, India

E-mail: info@blackeaglebooks.org
Website: www.blackeaglebooks.org

First International Edition Published by
Black Eagle Books, 2025

C R M
CONCEPTS & PRACTICES IN HOTEL AND TOURISM OPERATIONS
by **Bibhuti Bhushan Pradhan, Sasmita Mohanty and Ashish Mohanty**

Copyright © Authors

All rights reserved. No part of this publication may be reproduced, stored in a retrieval system, or transmitted, in any form or by any means, electronic, mechanical, photocopying, recording or otherwise without the prior permission of the publisher.

Cover & Interior Design: Ezy's Publication

ISBN- 978-1-64560-657-4 (Paperback)

Printed in the United States of America

CONTENTS

Chapter- I	
Genesis of Customer Relationship Management	11
Chapter-II	
CRM System	23
Chapter-III	
Multidimensional Approach in CRM	32
Chapter- IV	
CRM Scenario in Hospitality & Tourism Industry	44
Chapter-V	
Imprints of CRM In Hotel Industry	53
Chapter-VI	
Implementation of CRM In Business Enterprise	64
Chapter- VII	
Measurement Of CRM: Organisational Performance Perspective	73
Chapter-VIII	
Measurement Of CRM: Customers' Benefit Perspective	79
Chapter- IX	
Revolution in Hotel CRM: Use of Artificial Intelligence	86
Chapter- X	
Realizing the Benefits of CRM	97
Chapter- XI	
Establishing the Priorities for Effective CRM	106
Reference	117

Preface

The hospitality and tourism industries have witnessed unprecedented growth and competition in recent years as customers become increasingly discerning and tech-savvy, hotels, travel companies and tourism boards must adapt to meet their evolving needs and expectations. Customer Relationship Management (CRM) has emerged as a critical strategy for hospitality and tourism businesses to build loyalty, drive revenue, and gain a competitive edge.

This book aims to provide a comprehensive understanding of CRM principles and their application in the hospitality and tourism industries. Written for students, practitioners, and managers, this book explores the latest CRM concepts, technologies, and best practices, with a focus on hotel and tourism operations.

Through a combination of theoretical foundations, real-world industry examples, this book will equip readers with the knowledge and skills necessary to design, implement, and evaluate effective CRM strategies in hospitality and tourism settings. Whether you are a hospitality or tourism professional, educator, or student, this book will serve as a valuable resource for understanding the role of CRM in driving business success in these dynamic industries.

Acknowledgement

First and foremost, we would eternally thank the Almighty for giving us the strength and support in attempting to start this book project.

Many insights of this book are the valuable inputs of various authors and researchers from the field of academics and the industry. We take immense pride in acknowledging their contributions in enriching our manuscript and express our sincere indebtedness and gratitude to them.

We would like to take the opportunity of expressing my sincere thanks to the team of Black Eagle Books for giving us the opportunity to write this book. Especially, the professional staff, including the design and marketing team, were crucial in transforming a manuscript into a book ready for readers. We are sure that this book will serve its purpose and help the aspirants in understanding the theories and concepts of customer relationship management in hotel and tourism industry and gain valuable insights to apply them in the practical scenario. However, some errors might have crept in at some stage despite our best efforts. We hope the reader will appreciate the book. Suggestions for improving the text are most welcome.

Thank you all once again for your contributions in making this book a reality.

CHAPTER – I

Genesis of Customer Relationship Management

"Implementing a CRM system will do absolutely nothing for your business. However, the continued and effective use of it will." – **Bobby Darnell**, *Time for Dervin – Living Large in Geiggityville.*

Introduction

Customer Relationship Management (CRM) is one of those wonderful notions that swept the business world in the 1990s, promising to permanently change the way small and large firms interacted with their customers. Newer software systems and enhanced tracking tools, on the other hand, have dramatically increased CRM capabilities in recent years, and the promise of CRM is becoming a reality. With the introduction of newer, more customizable Internet solutions, competition has driven prices down to the point where even small firms can benefit from some custom CRM programmes.

Database marketing emerged in the 1980s as a catchphrase to describe the practice of forming customer care groups to speak to all of a company's clients personally. It was a helpful tool for keeping the lines of communication open and adapting service to the needs of larger, essential clients.

Companies began to strengthen CRM in the 1990s by making it more of a two-way street. Instead of simply collecting data for their own use, they began rewarding their consumers not only with better customer service, but also with incentives, gifts, and other perks in exchange for their loyalty. This was the start of the now-famous frequent flyer programmes, credit card bonus points, and a slew of additional resources based on CRM tracking of consumer activity and spending habits. CRM was now being utilised to drive sales both passively and actively through improved customer service.

CRM is based on relationship marketing principles, therefore understanding the evolution of CRM requires a quick overview of marketing history. Changes in market demand and competition intensity have resulted in a transition from transaction marketing to relationship marketing as sectors have grown. To exploit market demand, concepts such as 'the marketing mix' were developed in the 1950s. The '4Ps,' or product, pricing, promotion, and place,' were shorthand for the levers that, when pushed correctly, would lead to greater demand for the company's offer. The goal of this 'transactional' marketing approach was to create strategies that would maximise sales by maximising marketing mix spend.

Some of these fundamental marketing tenets were progressively questioned in the latter half of the twentieth century. In comparison to the 1950s, the market was dramatically different. Many markets had matured to the point where growth was slow or non-existent, putting a strain on business profitability. Consumers and customers were becoming more sophisticated and less receptive to traditional marketing forces, notably advertising, in many cases. As a result of globalisation of markets and new sources of competition, as well as the advent of new media and channels, customers had more options and convenience. To confront the challenges of this new competitive climate, creative business thought and action was required.

A new view is proposed on organisational performance and success based on relationships, in which the traditional marketing approach – based on the marketing mix –repositioned as the toolbox for understanding and responding to all of the significant players in a company's environment, rather than being replaced. It emphasises the value of a relationship-based approach to stakeholders. Marketing is still considered as a series of connected but segregated operations separate from the rest of the company in many large industrial organisations. By balancing the opposing interests of customers, employees, shareholders, and other stakeholders, relationship marketing aims to modify this perspective. It redefines the term "market" to mean a situation in which competing interests are made public and hence more easily regulated. In effect, marketing is assigned as primary responsibility for the company's market performance. Relationship marketing is defined by researchers as:
- a shift from functional to cross-functional marketing
- a method that addresses multiple 'market domains,' or stakeholder groups – not simply the traditional consumer market
- A transition away from marketing operations that focus solely on customer acquisition to marketing

actions that focus on both client retention and acquisition.

Relationship marketing is defined as acquiring, sustaining, and enhancing client connections in multi-service firms. It encompasses all marketing actions aimed at building, developing, and maintaining successful relational exchanges.

Academicians claimed in the 1950s that a focus on the 4P marketing mix was no longer the prevailing marketing logic and that Relationship Marketing (RM) might be a more appropriate new paradigm for marketing thought, theory, and practice. A larger emphasis was placed on Relationship Marketing, which served as the theoretical foundation for the development of customer relationship management.

Since market orientation primarily focused on collecting, analysing, and disseminating large quantities of customer data, modern management dutifully focused on relationship management, which specifically included one-to-one marketing techniques, which helped to create the opportunity for CRM practice. The rapid expansion of CRM can be linked to major causes such as severe commercial competition for valuable clients, the economics of customer retention, and technology advancements.

In the early 1990s, the first CRM initiatives were established. They primarily concentrated on call centre activities, which were later expanded to encompass sales and the creation of new channels. CRM originated as a result of firms adopting a customer-centric corporate philosophy and culture in order to support effective marketing, sales, and service activities that enabled effective customer relationships, customer happiness, and customer loyalty. CRM was purposefully established as an approach centered on gain, a 360-degree perspective of the customer, having all the data from all touchpoints, sustaining great customer relationships, improving customer loyalty, and enhancing customer lifetime value.

Concept of Customer Relationship Management

CRM is a crucial technique for customer management and marketing. CRM's growth is fueled by two key factors. The first is that client acquisition and retention have risen to the top of management's agenda. This extra dimension of corporate strategy has not emerged solely as a result of the ideas being espoused by systems vendors and management consulting organisations. As a result, management understand that CR is a competitive strategic dimension, if handled properly, can result in increased profit, but if poorly managed, may result in the loosing key customers, missed opportunities for customer development, and higher acquisition of customer and management costs. These factors may have an impact on company's profitability.

The second factor driving CRM growth is the move toward e-business and the growing importance of the Internet as a customer service and sales channel, which has left businesses feeling unsure. Many businesses have experienced extremely high client acquisition costs as a result of poor value model identification. The addition of a new channel has caused issues with existing channels. Companies have been looking for ways to connect old and new ways of managing customers, with a growing demand for an integrated view of the customer and a shift in IT investment from back-office efficiency to front-office effectiveness.

Although CRM is not a new concept, but it has gained practical importance as a result of current development in organization software technology. Relationship marketing is the heart of CRM, and information aims to improve clients' success by shifting from the traditional transactional marketing approach.

CRM was created due to fact that the customers have different tastes and purchasing habits. So, to expand the customer base and profits, organisations must modify their products by studying customer's motivation behind the choices. Because today's marketing landscape is very saturated and competitive, CRM is garnering a lot of attention in the business world.

CRM is a company-focused initiative that encompasses all sections inside a company. It is a tool that mines all the data from the customer's interaction points, creating and enabling the business to have a full view of the customer. As a result, businesses are able to identify and categorise the correct kind of clients, as well as forecast their future purchasing patterns". CRM is sometimes characterised as an all-encompassing strategy that integrates sales, customer service, marketing, field support, and other customer-facing departments.

Total quality management theories and new technical models formed and affected the present customer relationship management idea. Although all versions embrace the same core concept: customer connection, customer management, marketing strategy, client retention, and personalization, there is an apparent obscurity in the definition of customer relationship management. CRM's widely accepted goal is to help businesses provide better service to their consumers by implementing dependable systems and procedures for communicating with them.

An effective CRM strategy cannot be implemented in today's competitive corporate climate by simply installing and integrating a software package meant to support CRM operations. For a CRM policy to be effective and efficient, it must take a holistic approach. This strategy entails employee training, business process modifications based on customer needs, by adopting relevant IT systems (including software and sometimes hardware) and/or the use of IT-Services that allow the organisation or corporation to implement its CRM strategy. The main areas of concentration include service automation, personal data collection and processing, and self-service. It aims to combine and automate a company's different customer-serving activities.

Customer Relationship Management has grown to prominence as a crucial theme in less than a decade. Although the term CRM (now known as customer management) was coined in the late 1990s, the concept is in existence since its inception. It is founded on the concepts of Relationship Marketing (RM), which have been researched informally for about two decades but whose roots, involving the formation of mutually advantageous relationships between suppliers and customers, can be traced all the way back to the beginning of company. However, a number of major trends have evolved over the previous decade that collectively create the opportunity to better serve clients through information-enabled relationship marketing, or CRM. It can increase outstanding service at a lesser cost in situations when a profitable relationship already exists. Furthermore, it assists in meeting customers' unspoken wants. Customers have five basic needs: a) service, b) price, c) quality, d) action, and e) appreciation.

These apart, there will be demands that even customers may not have considered, but which, if met, would result in increased client loyalty. CRM, if used correctly, can lead to product and service cross-selling and up-selling. Selling the proper product to the right consumer is referred to as cross-selling. Another important feature of CRM is its potential to assist clients in repairing their egos. If done correctly, this calms the customer's unpleasant feelings that may have arisen as a result of the product or service failing to meet his expectations.

When it comes to aligning a firm with a customer relationship model, there are three major factors to consider: 1. The first is client retention: if the existing customers can be retained, then a firm will most likely grow and succeed in the future. Most firms only receive a little percentage of each customer's share. 2. The second is to create client potential: which entails converting one of the occasional casual customers into a higher-spending, more frequent, and referring advocate. 3. The third is customer de-selection: it is arguably the most contentious in de-selection of customers where it begins to lose those customers who do not provide long-term future value.

Integration of Relationship Marketing with Customer Relationship Management

A key element of CRM is relationship marketing, which places an emphasis on enduring client loyalty and involvement above transient objectives like new customer acquisition and one-off purchases. Relationship marketing creates deep, even emotional, relationships between a product and its customers that can result in recurring sales, unpaid word-of-mouth advertising, and customer data that can yield leads. The newest and most conventional marketing strategy, relationship marketing, is primarily concerned with increasing the quantity of individual purchases. The return on investment for client acquisition costs could not be sufficient under the transactional paradigm. After being convinced to pick a brand once, a customer could not do so again if there is no strong relationship marketing strategy in place.

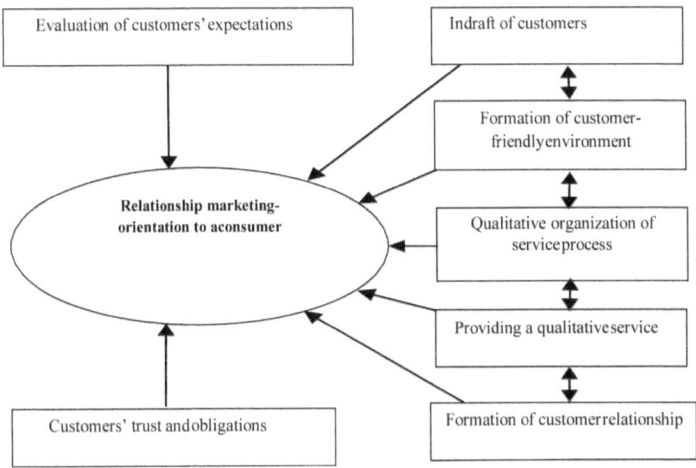

Figure 1
Relationship Marketing as the basis of CRM
Source: Rūta Urbanskienė, Daiva Žostautienė, Virginija Chreptavičienė (2008). The Model of Creation of Customer Relationship Management (CRM) System. Engineering Economics.

The New Age Customer

People have observed a massive client transformation in the new millennium. The importance of the consumer has become increasingly apparent in modern enterprises. Modern institution builders have also learned that the cultivation of customer relationships, rather than finance, technology, or labour, is the most important factor in an enterprise's success. According to academics, "excellent customer relations is the most important feature of a successful organisation." Customers are the most important factor in the effective operation of a business for modern sellers of goods and services. Economic liberalisation and globalisation have resulted in a multitude of goods and services in today's business climate.

Public enterprises are under tough competition from private enterprises in the age of economic liberalisation. Practically, competition has aided consumption development in all aspects of human life. The phenomenal increase in purchasing power of the people has also given an impetus to consumption. In the age of new consumerism, management has been adopting a 'marketing approach' against the traditional producing and selling approach. The contemporary marketing philosophy is a customer-oriented concept as compared to the product-oriented approach of traditional selling methods.

Modern clients are fully informed about the availability of goods and services across the globe in the age of the information and communication revolution. Consumers today don't take things for granted and fight for their rights and privileges. Over time, a number of consumer protection organisations, initiatives, and platforms have sprung up. Judicial and media institutions have also played an important role in safeguarding consumer interests.

Over time, the service business has likewise risen by leaps and bounds. Consumerism has been represented in a number of public-sector projects. In today's firms, consumer grievance redress systems are in place. Consumer grievances have been given priority in print and electronic media, and consumer-specific services have been supplied to generate greater awareness and responsibility among service providers toward consumers.

Our eagerness to consider the customer as an important person has driven us to give him various titles. The customer has been described variously as King,

Master, VIP, Guest and so on. These titles only reflect the desire of management to put the customer on a pedestal so that those who have the responsibility to serve them would feel adequate motivation. The customer is the most important partner because without him there is no business. Management may arrange capital and labor but it is the customer who throws in the sales revenue and makes it possible for the business to earn profits. There is a widespread belief that the customer is the profit, the rest is all overheads.

Customer-centric goods and services, as well as innovative marketing communication tactics, have helped firms adapt to the needs of new generation customers. Customers of today have evolved into engaged global citizens who are more aware of their worth, rights, and privileges. Customers in the new millennium are worried about the environment, social responsibility, human values, animal welfare, and other humanitarian aspects of product and service development.

Goods and service providers are also aware of their corporate social responsibility, non-price variables, and the intangibles involved in attracting and retaining customers. People's empowerment has become a difficult undertaking in our time. Customers must be empowered at all levels, and service providers must establish a strategic marketing approach that considers social obligations, demography, constitutional norms, governmental restrictions, evolving technology, and new millennium customers' developing desires.

Conclusion

The concepts underpinning CRM are not new, despite the name being relatively recent. Companies have used customer relationship management in one form or another for a very long time. The ability for businesses to manage one-to-one relationships with each of their thousands or millions of clients is what distinguishes modern CRM. CRM, or customer relationship management, is essentially a rethinking of relationship marketing ideas as they relate to maintaining customer relationships. The main distinction is that these principles are now implemented in the context of unparalleled technology innovation and market disruption.

CHAPTER – II

CRM Systems

"Our business is about technology, yes. But it is also about operations and customer relatinoships." – **Michael Dell.**

Introduction

The system that combines the creation and administration of marketing firms with the management of client groups is known as the customer relationship management system. It may be defined as a multimedia system that ensures the seamless integration of all technology resources utilised by a business with customer-related domains of activity. This company approach aims to enhance customer relationships while optimising profitability, income, and addressing customer wants. It is designed to provide maximum individualised client pleasure.

Businesses that handle customer relationships gain these kinds of clients, who are helpful in another roundabout way—that is, in generating revenue. Customers who aid in spreading awareness of the business, its operations, and the goods and services it offers are crucial. A well-planned and effective customer service strategy ensures that a customer will be more understanding in the event of a misunderstanding as well as more understanding if the consumer is not entirely pleased with the calibre of the product or service.

Types of CRM Systems

CRM systems come in four primary varieties: analytical, collaborative, strategic, and operational. Each is made to achieve a certain corporate objective. Numerous companies utilise several CRM systems, or they create a unique CRM solution that incorporates features from each system. These four CRM systems vary in the following ways:

Strategic CRM: It is a customer-centric business approach that focuses on attracting and retaining lucrative clients. Strategic CRM is a complicated set of actions that, when combined, establish the foundation for a long-term, difficult-to-copy competitive advantage. Strategic CRM is used to design interactions between companies and customers in order to maximise customers' lifetime value. It also recognises variances in customers' economic worth to the company as well as their expectations from the company. Value proposition, business case, customer strategy, enterprise transportation plan, and other stakeholders are all features of a defined CRM strategy.

Operational CRM: It is concerned with the automation of customer-facing processes like sales, marketing, and customer service. It helps to interact between a company, its channels, and its customers. It enables customers to contact the company and facilitates collaboration among suppliers, partners, and customers. It helps in improving customer care, internet marketing, and sales force automation, among other things. Through automation procedures, consumer communication & processing become easier. In marketing, sales, and service, it controls and synchronises consumer interactions. Customer data is collected through a variety of channels, including call centres, contact management systems, mail, fax, sales force, and the web. The information is then structured and saved in a customer-centric database that is accessible to all individuals who interact with the client. The contact centre and contact management are two typical operational CRMs.

Analytical CRM: It is concerned with the intelligent mining of customer-related data for strategic or tactical goals. Building data warehouses, developing relationships, analysing data, and so on all require analytical CRM. It makes use of consumer data to create a win-win situation between a company and its customers. Analysis, modelling, and assessment aid in the optimization of data sources for a better knowledge of client behaviour and a more tailored encounter. Customer happiness is critical for boosting a company's competitiveness and attaining customer goals. It must be improved by identifying client needs and expectations and ensuring that they are met. This necessitates the development of a measurement system that is fed by data, some of which will be provided directly by the client and some of which will be collected from the company's computer system. In order to develop customer profiles, discover behaviour patterns, establish satisfaction levels, and enable customer segmentation, data contained in the contact centric database is evaluated using a variety of analytical techniques. The analytical CRM's information and knowledge will aid in the development of appropriate marketing and promotion tactics.

Collaborative CRM: It uses technology to optimise

company, partner, and customer value across organisational boundaries. According to Kracklauer and Mills (2004), CRM systems are connected with enterprise-wide systems to enable enhanced customer responsiveness throughout the supply chain. Instant service response based on customer input, one-to-one solutions to client requirements, direct online connections with consumers at any time and from any location, and customer care centres that assist customers with their questions are among the characteristics. Increased client happiness, personalised service, and attracting and retaining consumers are some of the effects.

Benefits of Customer Relationship Management System

Currently, the majority of businesses acknowledge the clear benefits of CRM, and nearly all of them either employ particular CRM technologies to support their operations or assess the benefits of CRM technology in detail and make plans for its eventual implementation.

Benefits to Owner

One of the benefits an owner gets is the decrease in costs in managing customers and decrease in automation of routine works. This apart, the CRM system also helps in increasing the income level due to quality of sales and services.

Benefits to Customer

The benefits a customer stands to gain from an effective CRM system is that they are made to feel important with timely information on various services on offer. A customer can decide upon an offer that is appropriate and adequate as well.

Benefits to Employee

The system needs to be friendly; it makes it possible to do more tasks at once, and doing so is linked to a greater compensation. It also fosters self-control, the ability to take the lead, and healthy competition.

Three Pillars of Customer Relationship Management

CRM is a combination of three pillars namely Customer, Relationship & Management.

Customer: Customers are the key source of the company's current profit and future growth in modern enterprises. Because buying decisions are typically a collaborative activity among participants in the decision-making process, it can be difficult to tell who is the genuine consumer. Customers can be distinguished and managed with the help of information technology. CRM can be conceived as a marketing strategy based on customer data. Customers have five needs: Service, Price, Quality, Action, and Appreciation.

Relationship: In today's competitive business world, modern firms cannot exist without active customer appreciation, participation, and success. In reality, a company's relationship with its customers entails constant bi-directional communication and involvement. Short-term or long-term relationships, continuous or discrete relationships and repeated or one-time relationships are all possibilities. Relationships can be behavioural or attitudinal. Customers have a positive opinion about the company and its products, but their purchasing decisions are very situational.

Management: It is the responsibility of organisational leaders to help organisations and customers build mutually beneficial relationships. From the standpoint of business promotion, maintaining a rewarding, fruitful, and long-term relationship between clients and service providers becomes a difficult challenge. The consumer data gathered is translated into business knowledge, which leads to activities that make use of the data and market prospects.

Installing and integrating a software package meant to assist CRM procedures cannot be a successful CRM strategy in today's competitive corporate climate. For a CRM policy to be effective and efficient, it must take a holistic approach. This strategy entails employee training, business process modifications based on customer needs, the adoption of relevant IT systems (including software and maybe hardware) and/or the use of IT-Services that allow the organisation or corporation to implement its CRM strategy.

Integrated Customer Relationship Management Processes

CRM is an amalgam of several customer-focused management strategies that facilitates the development of enduring relationships with customers. Numerous corporate functions, including data warehousing, sales force automation, data mining, decision support, and reporting tools, are aided by CRM systems. CRM primarily comes in three flavours: analytical, collaborative, and operational solutions. The operational CRM system makes advantage of efficiency gains and automation. While the collaborative CRM system is used to manage and connect communication channels and customer engagement touchpoints, the analytical CRM system is used to analyse customer data. Technology primarily manages successful customer relationship management, which includes both front- and back-office systems, by analysing the data. While the back-office conducts analysis, the front office ensures that clients' information is continuously exchanged. The literature on relationship marketing serves as the main theoretical basis for CRM research. Developing and maintaining relationships with current clients is the first step. Recognising that connections change as the CRM process progresses is the second component. The organisation is impacted by the third way that relationships evolve, and businesses are expected to manage their interactions and connections with consumers differently at each step. The fourth factor is the non-homogeneous distribution of the relationship value to the business. The CRM integrated diagram is mentioned below.

Fig 2
Integrated CRM

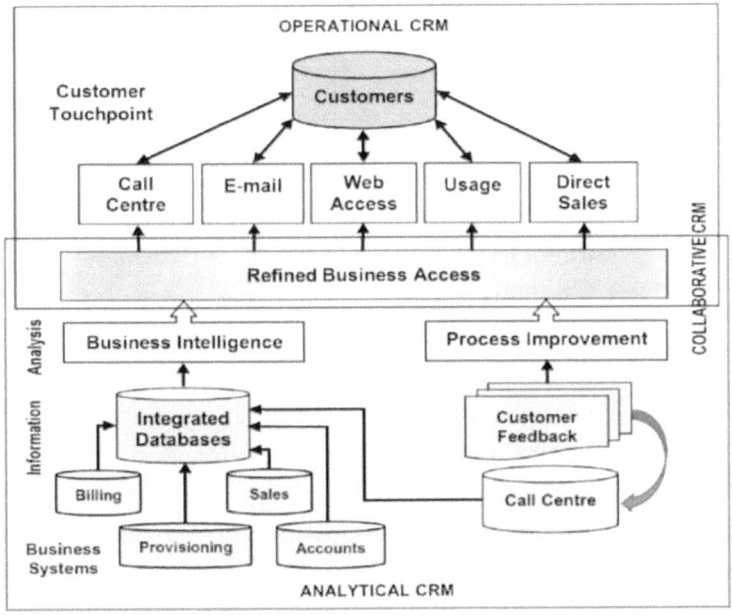

Source: Saha et al., 2021 (*Amalgamation of Customer Relationship Management and Data Analytics in Different Business Sectors—A Systematic Literature Review, Sustainability*).

Goals of Customer Relationship Management

Customer relationship management is a well-thought practice in any business operations that is carried out on a long-term planning with an objective of maximizing profits, enhancing revenue, maximizing satisfaction of customers. The primary goal of operational practices in a hotel using customer relationship management is to create a long-term relationship with the customers by understating their needs, wants, choices and expectations.

Fig 3
Evolving Phase of CRM

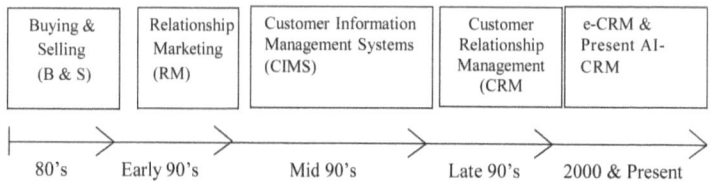

Objectives of Customer Relationship Management

CRM is primarily focused on three goals:
1. To increase income per client by better understanding and serving one's customers.
2. To integrate data from numerous channels held in disparate systems to improve customer satisfaction and retention.
3. To reduce customer acquisition and service expenses by automating, managing, and analysing processes and data using technology.

Many businesses are recognising that a stronger client relationship is critical to their success. As a result, they are bringing their consumers and their extended enterprise business units closer together. CRM objectives can help you boost your business opportunities:

- The right customers are targeted, and a progressive

communication strategy is employed, with each customer receiving the relevant offers through the appropriate channel and time.

There are various reasons why performance review is highly helpful in organisation improvement for which a framework of CRM effectiveness is necessary. To begin with, measurement removes the uncertainty and disagreement that can develop when debating high-level strategic concepts. Second, measuring provides the organisation with the precise vocabulary it requires to convey what it wants to accomplish and how it intends to accomplish it at all levels. Third, measuring allows for continuous evaluation of the organization's alignment with strategic objectives. Last but not least, measuring not only increases but also accelerates the rate of change. The four viewpoints are customer understanding, interaction, value, and satisfaction.

Conclusion

The term "customer relationship management system" refers to a system that combines relationship marketing company formation and administration with customer group management. Since customer relationship management cannot be limited to merely illustrating relationships, it is imperative that relationship marketing theory be applied to a more limited understanding of the field. It is far more crucial to comprehend the management and development of associations and relationships.

CHAPTER – III

Multidimensional Approach in CRM

"On average, sales and marketing costs average from 15%-35% of total corporate costs. So, the effort to automate for more sales efficiency is absolutely essential. In cases reviewed, sales increase due to advanced CRM technology have ranged from 10% to more than 30%." – **Harvard Business Review**.

Introduction

CRM has no commonly accepted definition. It's a topic that's been approached from a variety of angles (e.g., strategy, philosophy and technology). Depending upon various circumstances and variables, it is perceived differently by individuals. On the basis of literature reviews and extensive interviews with select managers of various organisations, it was claimed that customer relationship management is a multi-dimensional construct comprising four behavioural dimensions that are: Customer Orientation, CRM organisation, Knowledge Management, and Technology-based CRM. These dimensions must work in tandem to improve the performance of an organization. Thus, the findings of research support the idea that for the successful implementation of CRM it is the People, Processes, Technology and Strategy are essential. The impact of CRM aspects on call centres was explored and was found out that the customer orientation is an important aspect of CRM that is more comprehensive than just focusing on customer only. Several studies have emphasised the critical importance of customer orientation as an important facet of CRM that has been steadily extended to the service sector to improve the bonding between service organisations and their customers. Successful external marketing increased satisfaction of customer, and improved overall performance are all dependent on an organization's improved sense of client orientation.

Dimensions of CRM

As per the previous studies on people, strategy, processes and technology, it has been decided to employ the similar aspects of CRM – "Customer Orientation, CRM Organisation, Knowledge Management and Technology-based CRM, as they firmly link to the core components of customer relationship management".

Customer Orientation Dimension

Customer Orientation refers to an employee's willingness to meet the demands of customers; it has a beneficial impact on employee performance as well as customer satisfaction. It can help to uphold a positive relationship between the service provider and the customers, resulting in an increase in the company's performance. In research, stronger customer-oriented behaviours in businesses have been found to have a significant influence on the performance of business with long-term customer satisfaction and loyalty. It is suggested that managers must focus on customer-centric strategy that aligns to societal norms, structure of the organisation and employee performance and rewards. At the same time, the image of the hotel is enhanced when its employees provide excellent service is directly proportional to process fit. Hotel managers attempt to maximise company results by growing and enhancing profitability because of the dynamic market environment and competitive environment of hotel industry. As a result, focusing on the consumer may be the most effective strategy for improving performance of organization. Marketing literature assumes that incorporating customer orientation will improve organisational performance in this case. A customer-centric strategy has been linked to an organization's performance in numerous studies. In brief, the customer-orientation strategy is an important aspect of CRM and a valuable resource for the company. As a result, in order to successfully use CRM and gain a competitive edge, businesses must have a customer-centric culture.

Customer orientation was identified to be an important aspect in the successful deployment of CRM, its primary goal is to promote lasting satisfaction and loyalty of customers. Furthermore, recent studies have shown that service businesses, such as hotels, must have a better clarity on customer orientation as it improves their performances. The interaction between service providers and the service encounter occurs in a hotel, just as it does in other service-oriented companies. Because consumption and delivery of a hospitality product occur at the same time, the determinant of quality service is largely dependent on the individual delivering the service. The experience made during such an encounter will contribute to customer satisfaction and decide how long the experience will be remembered by a customer. As a result, in order to improve the client experience, hotels must focus on customer engagement and ensure that the quality service is constantly provided. A positive relationship between the consumer and the service provider might help to achieve customer orientation. Customer orientation, according to research, leads to improved organisational performance. This could be because it aids the company's understanding of its clients. There is a link between client orientation and marketing planning competencies. Marketing planning capabilities ensure that action and innovative oriented marketing initiatives are implemented successfully.

CRM Organization Dimension

CRM deployment may fail if an organisation is devoid of a culture based on the establishment of long-term customer relationships since the organisation is prepared. Companies must create a service-oriented culture for professionals to demonstrate customer-oriented behaviour with regards to providing them with latest tools and technology, systems to track customer satisfaction and customer complaints, reward scheme, and above all an inspirational leader to motivate and support them. An organisation can accomplish desirable staff customer-orientation behaviours based on these principles. Focusing on key clients embedded in an organization's CRM system. The entire firm must be oriented around cultivating these lucrative relationships. CRM, on the other hand, will not be successful unless the project is fully integrated into the business, although the organisations achieve the cutting-edge technology and attempt to create a customer-focus orientation. As a result, successful CRM adoption necessitates reorganising organisational structure and processes, involving all employees of organisation in the project, and appropriately directing change. As a result, organisational structure must also promote collaboration between functional areas because CRM data is helpful if it is efficiently transmitted to all pertinent domains. Furthermore, the organisational hierarchy is crucial to the successful deployment of CRM and, as a result, increases the performance of a business.

CRM is highly dependent on staff attitude, dedication, and performance in the hotel sector; marketplace success necessitates the growth of business through employee commitment and motivation. In view of this, the achievement of CRM depends on good systems or technology as well as good philosophy in service and appropriate operational methods. Numerous researches demonstrated that customer relationship management has a favourable link with an establishment's performance in this situation.

Organizations must provide an adequate working environment to guarantee that service professionals practice behaviours that are oriented towards the customers only. This entails offering current tools and technology to employees, as well as tracking customer satisfaction and complaint management systems, inspiring leadership, and appropriate compensation schemes. CRM will not be successful unless the project fully integrates people, despite the fact that organisations have customer and technology driven approach. CRM success also necessitates a strong service philosophy as well as appropriate operating procedures. To properly adopt CRM and, as a result, increase organisational performance, all of the organization's resources must be utilized. Marketing decisions like brand distinctiveness, price, communication, and distribution, may be influenced by the CRM organization in the future. In this regard, it has been revealed that several hotel chains smartly and flexibly fix their room tariff based on previously obtained consumer data.

Knowledge Management Dimension

Customer knowledge has been viewed as a significant organisational resource in recent years, and customer knowledge transmission strategies have been viewed as crucial resources that enables the organization to strengthen its customer relationship on a long-term perspective and help the organisation to attain an edge over its competitors. Furthermore, good CRM relies on properly converting client data into customer knowledge. Because the potential of knowledge is realised when shared throughout several areas of the company in order to address present and expected customer needs. And, the customer knowledge that is generated must be communicated across the organization. Knowledge management aids an organization's success by fostering effective customer interactions by impacting the organization performance. In light of this, it is emphasised the need for hospitality organisations to use knowledge management to improve their competitive advantage. The sector is transforming into a knowledge-intensive sector as a result of its extensive technology usage and characteristics of service products, which are dependent on the interaction between staff and consumers. As a result, activities centred on knowledge management are becoming increasingly important to hotels since they help improve personnel's understanding of specific consumer requirements. Organizations must gain new information about their consumers, research and use their existing knowledge, and communicate this knowledge across the firm in order to remain competitive. Numerous research has established a beneficial association between market effectiveness, knowledge management and financial performance, customer retention and customer satisfaction.

Furthermore, efficiently managing knowledge can assist an enterprise in successfully promoting healthier customer relationships, which can positively influence the performance of organization. As a result, it is believed that future research looks at the effect of the knowledge management construct on the hotel business. Given the scarcity of studies on the function of knowledge management in the hotel industry, this is strongly recommended. Customer knowledge management is closely linked to marketing capabilities, and it considerably aids firms in making decisions strategically to enhance organizational performance. Hence, the hotels need to embrace customer interaction in their culture to ensure the success of knowledge management.

Technology-based CRM Dimension

A state-of-art system can be employed to ameliorate the potential of companies to lower internal costs, better interaction with the environment, and enhance the profit in the long run, due to improvements in information communication technology (ICT). By and large, hotels in various categories have found out the need to use sophisticated CRM systems. In this context, it is believe that if the IT is not used correctly in the process, strategy of CRM will fail to produce the desired results. Furthermore, one of the most significant prospects in the hotel business is the usage of technological advancements strategically in marketing functions, because it is critical to make correct decisions by accessing the right information at appropriate time from employees to provide the best services. Furthermore, maintaining connections with customers by integrating, sharing and enabling data, managing customer-organization interactions, data analysis of customer are the products of effective and efficient CRM. In addition, it is found out that hotels have utilised ICT as a tool for dealing with dynamic surroundings as a result of increased competitiveness and customer expectations. Numerous studies support this claim, that CRM technology positively impacts performance of organization.

If information technology is not leveraged appropriately, CRM strategies would fail. Similarly, it is pertinent for the hotels to use the technology effectively to elicit and synthesize information from their employees to offer services to customers by making appropriate decisions. The CRM technology construct is inextricably linked to hotel organization performance. This is due to the fact that new technologies are regarded as the primary drivers of change. Several studies have found that various customer-centric initiatives are unable to fulfil their objectives sans IT assistance. As a result, CRM-based technology enables businesses to design and execute successful marketing campaigns aimed at keeping consumers and increasing profits.

Figure 4

Source: Four elements of CRM system (adjusted according to Sin, Tse, Yim., 2005)

CRM as a Cross- Functional Process

Cross-functional cooperation is necessary for successful customer relationship management, encompassing not only marketing but the whole company. In order to create a cross-functional approach to customer relationship management, it is necessary to first identify the critical processes that demand attention, and then to identify the critical questions or concerns that each of these processes requires the organisation to solve. Viewed as a strategic collection of processes or activities, customer relationship management starts with a thorough analysis of an organization's strategy (the strategy development process) and ends with improved business outcomes and increased shareholder value (the performance assessment process). The foundation of any successful relationship is the understanding that competitive advantage originates from the act of creating value—both for the firm and the client. In order to create a better customer experience at every touchpoint where the customer and supplier interact, all significant businesses will engage in customer relationship management activities that involve gathering and intelligently using customer and other pertinent data (the information management process) (the multi-channel integration process).

Figure 5
CRM as Cross-Functional Process

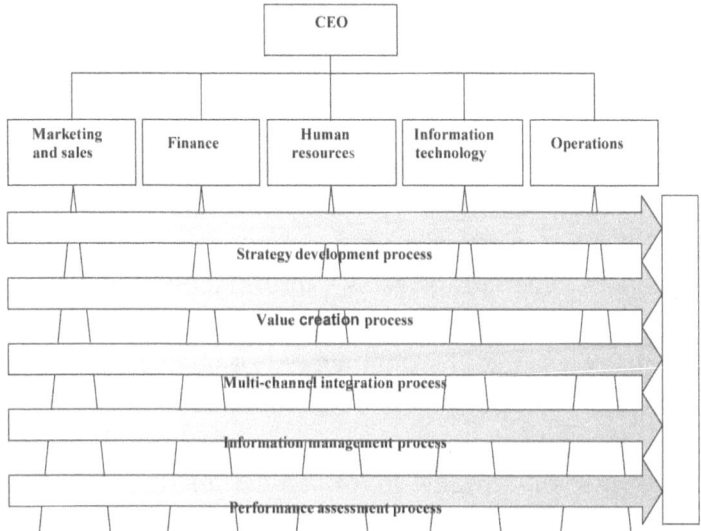

Source: Arian Payne, Achieving Excellence in Customer Management, Elsevier, Oxford, 2005

Practices of CRM

CRM is a method of establishing an active, participatory, and interactive relationship between a company and its customers. The real goal is to gain a 360-degree perspective of customers and be able to predict and respond to their requirements with focused and successful actions at every customer touch point. It is well known that acquiring a new customer costs five times as much as keeping an existing customer. Focusing on the consumer has become critical to surviving in this global and competitive economy. CRM methods teach employees that no matter where, when, or how a customer interacts with them, the contact should be individualised, consistent, and show that the organisation recognises and values them.

CRM techniques involve a variety of approaches for preserving customer relationships, such as putting the customer at the centre of organisational action by offering technical support and having a comprehensive picture of the client's needs and requirements. Hotels employ a variety of procedures, but each time new ones are devised after listening to clients in order to encourage them to return to the same organisation.

CRM has an impact on a variety of functions inside a business, including sales, information technology, operations, marketing, and finance. CRM will almost certainly necessitate the deployment of new technologies, which will necessitate a re-examination of business processes that should guide technological decisions. Many firms still struggle to implement a successful CRM programme because they let software dictate their customer management strategy or retrofit their customer strategy to match the CRM technology they purchased. CRM software must not only integrate functionally at the front office but also with back-office tasks such as manufacturing and billing.

Practices of customer relationship management in service-oriented sectoral focused organisations are carried out on the following dimensions: managing customer needs, satisfying customers, acquiring customers, fulfilling expectations of the customer and their commitment, managing employee satisfaction, leadership and management and technological support.

Conclusion

The capacity of construction companies to innovate their marketing and gain a competitive edge may be enhanced by the completion of CRM dimensions, which in turn can build lifetime value based on durable relationships. Contrary to the conventional view, a multidimensional approach to CRM yields outcomes that can assist practitioners and construction businesses in customising their CRM practices and overcoming obstacles related to organisational and technological CRM preparedness.

CHAPTER - IV

CRM Scenario in Hospitality & Tourism Industry

"Integrity is important in building relationships. And is the foundation upon which many other qualities for success are built, such as respect, dignity and trust." – **John C. Maxwell**

Introduction

Tourism is a multi-dimensional industry made up of various sectors related to virtually all areas of the economy. This sun rise industry has captured an increasingly significant position in the global economy. Tourism enjoys a distinguished position owing to its immense business opportunities and close linkages to the transport and accommodation industry and a host of other sectors. In recent years, virtually every tourist destination has taken steps to increase the number of visitors. The revolutionary developments in air travel and technological resources such as GDS and Internet have provided new opportunities for countries and individual tourism firms to promote tourism, both within and across borders. The increase in rising incomes and leisure time are also key factors attributed to the phenomenal growth in the tourism sector.

One of the industries in India with the quickest rate of growth is tourism. The industry has a major effect on employment and propels regional development. It also boosts the performance of industries that are associated. India's tourism and hospitality sector is expected to bring in more than $59 billion by 2028. Additionally, it is projected that by 2028, there would be 30.5 million foreign tourist arrivals (FTAs). The Ministry of Tourism allocates more than half of its budget towards the development of megaprojects, circuits, destinations, and infrastructure projects related to rural tourism. In 2023, the hotel accommodation and revenue are expected to reach $7.66 billion. By 2027, there would be 61.3 million potential clients at a CAGR of 8.29%. 8,59,688 foreign visitors arrived in March 2024 compared to 7,95,827 in March 2023 and 9,78,236 in March 2019, representing increases of 8.0% and -12.1%, respectively, over 2023 and 2019. Arrivals of foreign tourists from January to March 2024 were 28,21,085, up from 25,29,766 in January to March 2023 and 31,79,792 in January to March 2019, respectively. This is an increase of 11.5% and -11.3% over 2023 and 2019.

Customer Relationship Management in Tourism Industry

Customer relationship management in tourism is essentially about building long- term and mutually beneficial relationships with tourists. While providing services to tourists, the dynamics of building relationships with them takes on a different dimension due to the very nature of service offerings. The nature of tourism services makes it difficult for customer relationship managers to design, deliver and manage its quality. Tourism organizations are found to devote most of their time and expenditure to attract new customers while efforts to retain the existing customers are not very seriously planned. It is equally important for the tourism firms to retain customers and not merely expand the list. Retaining the existing customers (tourists) forms the main theme of CRM. It gives more emphasis on attracting, maintaining, and enhancing customer relationships.

The direct contacts between marketers or service providers and tourists create opportunities for greater understanding, a better appreciation of needs as well as short falls and challenges, and emotional bonding; all of which facilitate building relationships. Tourism and the various related sectors are pioneering many of the CRM initiatives.

There are numerous service providers for each component of tourism and therefore customers have plenty of options to choose from. Customers are prone to switch over from one organization to another. Thus, there are needs and opportunities for tourism companies for attracting customers are building relationships with them. While promising quality service to tourists, organizations must ensure its prompt delivery. This is one of the ways for differentiating on dimensions of service that becomes meaningful to the tourists and difficult to imitate.

Process of Customer Relationship Management in Tourism Industry

Primarily, as regards CRM process in tourism, it is utmost important for firms to determine and focus on psychology of tourists. Destination planners and tour marketers must comprehensively attend to the *feelings* of tourists towards a particular destination / product / service. Furthermore, it is essential to influence the environmental forces that impact the decision – making of tourists. By analyzing tourists' buying behavior and patterns of purchase, tourism service providers are bound to gain competitive advantage.

They get a clear-cut understanding of the demand (market) and hence are able to offer customized services to tourists (supply). Destination developers and tourism companies must grasp the limitations the tourists have in terms of product / destination knowledge. In the context of tourism operations, the organizations need to engage the best strategies for effectively convincing the tourists. 'Conviction' is of supreme value for winning the hearts of customers. Honesty pays rich dividends while exaggerative claims and non-delivery or under-delivery of promises tend to backfire.

Customer Relationship Management and its Phases in Tourism Industry
Phase–I: Establishing Association with New Customers

In the first phase, tourism organizations need to acquire new customers / market segments or widen the customer base by promoting the destination offerings / packages / products and service leadership.

Phase – II: Elevating Association with Customers

In this phase, tourism companies enrich the relationships by offering premium products / services in a cost – effective fashion. Also, they create a platform for excellence in cross selling and up selling, thereby deepening and broadening the relationships

Phase- III: Retaining Customer Association and their Goodwill

CRM in tourism focuses on maintaining one-to-one relationships with tourists. In the third phase, adaptability is the factor which is highlighted. Tourism service adaptability is delivering what exactly individual customers prefer and not what the market requires.

Customer Satisfaction and Customer Retention in Tourism: The Role of CRM

In the travel and tourism sector, keeping existing clients is just as important as finding new ones. The expense of obtaining a new client can sometimes be five times more than that of keeping an existing one, as is often recognised. This is when having a strong CRM system is useful. Through the monitoring of consumer preferences, behaviours, and input, companies are able to provide tailored experiences that surpass customers' expectations. Increased client satisfaction and, eventually, customer retention result from this. Moreover, happy consumers frequently become brand ambassadors. By telling their networks about their wonderful experiences, they provide priceless word-of-mouth advertising that may draw in new clients.

Tourism Business & Important features of CRM

Customer relationship management systems are not all created equal. Certain elements are essential for efficiently maintaining consumer interactions in the tourist business. For your tourist business, the following characteristics of a CRM system are essential to consider:

Contact management: This aids in the organisation of all client data, encompassing contact details, demographics, historical exchanges, and more. It gives you access to a single source of truth about your clients, so you can provide them with superior service.

Bookings Management: You can track and manage all of your reservations in one location with an integrated booking management function, which lowers mistakes and boosts productivity.

Customer Segmentation: This function aids in the classification of clients according to various criteria, enabling you to focus your marketing efforts on particular categories.

Integration with Other Tools: To create a unified platform that boosts productivity, a strong CRM should interact easily with other marketing and sales tools.

Diagnostics and Reporting: This gauges the success of your marketing activities and offers insights into consumer behaviour. It supports you in making data-driven decisions that might strengthen your marketing plans and accelerate the expansion of your company.

It can be said that rapid changes in consumer purchasing patterns, technology advancements, competitive structures, service delivery methods, and distribution channels define the tourism business. Any tourism CRM program must adhere to a long-term, consistent policy regarding how customers are to be managed. This includes providing special experiences and treatment, improving the quality of services, knowledge management, implementing the newest technological practices, encouraging customers to co-create services, and creating outstanding customer loyalty programs. This demonstrates how the tourist industry's CRM paradigms may be improved by including high-quality service delivery practices that will undoubtedly surpass client expectations. The use of cutting-edge technical techniques like GPS and GDS has drastically altered CRM in the tourism industry.

Tourism organisations throughout the globe devote

a significant amount of time and resources to researching the requirements, desires, expectations, tastes, and preferences of their clientele. They will be able to identify important clients and create long-term retention plans by evaluating the data. However, relationship managers find it challenging to create, implement, and oversee the quality of CRM rules due to the nature of tourist services. CRM in the tourist industry places a high value on retaining and strengthening client connections as well as drawing in new business by boosting relationship programs. In the era of digital transformation, businesses are leveraging technology to streamline processes, enhance customer experiences, and drive growth. Among these technologies, Customer Relationship Management (CRM) has emerged as a game-changer, especially for customer-centric industries like tourism.

Multidimensional Communication in Hospitality and Tourism Industry: The CRM Way

Effective use of CRM and its features enables travel and hospitality companies to customise their products to the tastes of their clients. This increases income and sales while also fostering consumer loyalty. Systems for managing customer relationships have long been a crucial component of sales and marketing campaigns. Previously, though, their use was restricted to large corporations that needed assistance managing their operation centres and had robust on-premises networks. Businesses of all sizes are now utilising CRM and taking use of its advantages to efficiently manage, nurture, and convert leads as a result of the surge in digitisation. CRM software is being used by the hospitality sector as a whole to establish and preserve positive connections with visitors. Accurate guest data is accessible, allowing hotels to tailor their visitors' experiences while they are on site and offer more focused marketing between visits to boost repeat business. For example, you may use a guest's profile to customise their room settings when they arrive, or you can use it to set up automated SMS birthday messages or gift cards. A graphic is used to demonstrate a win-win strategy for the hotel and tourist industry, facilitating greater comprehension and consumption.

Fig. 6
Integrative Approach of CRM in Hospitality & Tourism Industry

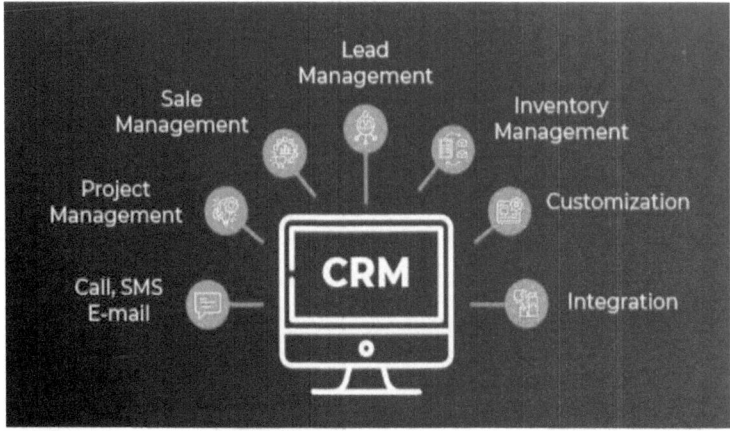

Source: www.routemobile.com

Conclusion

Customer relationship management, or CRM, has emerged as a key tool in the tourism industry, revolutionising how businesses interact with guests and nurture connections across the customer lifecycle. CRM, or customer relationship management, is essentially the systematic management of interactions and communications with tourists, from initial inquiry to post-trip assessment, with the ultimate goal of enhancing customer happiness, fostering loyalty, and encouraging repeat business. One of CRM's primary goals in the travel business is to centralise and organise customer data from several touchpoints and channels, including website queries, email exchanges, phone conversations, social media interactions, and booking histories.

By merging this data into a single system, travel agencies may create customised experiences and offers that appeal to specific travellers, giving them a comprehensive understanding of each client's preferences, past interactions, and activities. CRM solutions specifically designed for the tourism industry provide an array of features and functionalities aimed at streamlining tedious tasks, enhancing client interaction, and propelling sales and marketing campaigns. For example, CRM systems enable travel firms to segment their customer base based on booking trends, preferences, or demographics. As a result, more specialised marketing campaigns and communication strategies may be developed.

CHAPTER – V

Imprints of CRM in Hotel Industry

"CRM is your GPS to a better route on your Business Development journey." – **Bobby Darnell**

Introduction

In today's competitive marketplace, businesses must make every effort to stay afloat and manage customer relationships in order to succeed. Businesses have realized that customer relations are essential for their success. By implementing the appropriate processes in management and applying strategies that are customer-centric, customer relationship management (CRM) can enable companies to strengthen lasting relationship with customers to gain profits. CRM system emphasizes the development and retention of relationships with customers by integrating people, processes, and technology.

A significant component of the tourism business is the hotel industry. Historically viewed only as a foreign exchange earner and a luxury service provider, today the industry not only provides direct employment but also indirectly promotes both tourism and commerce. However, the challenges hotels face these days are increased globalization, increasing customer turner, rising customer acquisition costs, and a rise in customer expectations, which means that their competitiveness depends heavily on how well they satisfy the customers by understanding their needs and wants. The keys to success are managing client relationships and providing high-quality services that can lead to increased customer satisfaction. When it comes to the company's survival in competitions and, as a result, the development of the marketing plan, satisfied consumers become the key to the matter. Competitiveness is heavily reliant on hotels' ability to efficiently serve their clients, especially in the hotel industry, which has increased competition and high customer turnover.

Customer satisfactions are crucial components in the battle to acquire competitive advantage in the hotel business and the hotel sector as one of the most profitable and dynamic industries in the world today. Guests at the hotel come from a variety of backgrounds and have varying levels of personal experience. As a result, hotel visitors have varying expectations and impressions. Also, client expectations fluctuate and expand with time; just because a customer is satisfied now does not mean they will be satisfied in the future. Hence, the first and possibly most important step in satisfying customers is to understand and continue to meet their expectations. Customers are lost when corporations do not understand what customers want and rival companies meet their expectations. Hence, the hotel must be able to meet the needs and expectations of every customer in a high demand-driven market if they want to compete. Getting repeat customers and experiencing behavioral loyalty requires an understanding of the characteristics of business performance that influence them to continue to buy from a company. The technique of meticulously maintaining comprehensive data about each individual client and all of their touch points in order to maximise loyalty is known as customer relationship management. All consumer-business interactions are considered touch points. Businesses must adopt a customer-focused business strategy across the entire organisation as a critical competitive tactic, which entails putting the demands of the consumer first. One of the best methods to promote customer connection development, enhance service quality, and grow the client base is through a well-functioning CRM. Consequently, it will help to improve profitability and client retention. CRM's influence on the hotel sector can assist establishments maintain their competitiveness.

Hotels must understand what their consumers want and strive to continually enhance their services in order to satisfy them. They must employ the correct methods to collect and integrate consumer information in order to discover what customers want and render the services they anticipate. Furthermore, service organisations are inseparable aspects necessary to develop relationships with consumers because of their basic qualities of production and consumption. Furthermore, when compared to other industries, the hotel industry demands more client information and specialised services. This is for a matter of fact that the hotels have easy access to guest data as guests have to register their names and addresses during check-in along with passport information and further private details if they belong to a different country of origin. Furthermore, people often partake information pertaining to their choices and preferences with hotel employees to have a memorable stay, which is a perfect opportunity for hotels to use a combination of databases and information technology services to provide the best customer experience possible.

Organisations must apply a customer-focused business strategy throughout their entire set-up as a crucial competitive strategy, which implies they must focus on the demands of their customers. One of the most effective strategies to facilitate creating relationships with customers, enhancing service quality, and expanding the client base is to implement a good CRM. As a result, it will help to increase profitability and client loyalty. Further, CRM's impact on the hotel industry can help hotels stay competitive.

Therefore, it is imperative in today's times that the hotels should implement customer relationship management strategies that aim at seeking, gathering, validating and sharing appropriate information across the organization in order to increase profitability and guest satisfaction and loyalty. The hotel industry cannot endure without customers, as today's customers have various alternatives and options and their target customers are of prime importance to star hotels. In the hotel industry, customer care and service should be a top priority. Customer relationship management practice, especially at star hotels, is extremely difficult. Simply the installation and integration of software packages at star hotels will not lead to an effective and successful CRM strategy. It should be in sync with the company's operations, goals, and employee and customer acceptance. If star hotels build and maintain strong relationships with their guests, their competitors will find it difficult to replace them, giving them a long-term competitive edge. CRM in star hotels is a critical component for expanding a hotel's client base and volume of sales. The use of CRM allows hotels to handle entire areas of client contacts in a way that allows them to optimise profits from each customer. CRM assists businesses that create a lot of data about their customers. As a result, the importance of CRM strategies in service-sector organisations for establishing long-term client relationships is paramount and is an excellent fit for the hotel business, especially if applied correctly.

Furthermore, rising customer acquisition expenses, increased customer demands, cost conscious customers, a volatile market condition, and decreased brand loyalty are all major elements that encourage the adoption of CRM as a beneficial technique in hotels. If translated into customer knowledge and individualised services, the vast amount of data collected from each client by these organisations can be quite valuable. Therefore, CRM is one of the most effective mechanisms for enabling the growth of profitable long-term client connections, hence improving hotel performance and profitability.

In a competitive business environment, every customer's expectation and need must be met by the hotel industry. It is important on the part of the hotelier to decipher business performance indicators that motivates the customers to make repeat purchases and show their loyalty. Hence, modern hotels should also focus on the effective practice of CRM that aims to seek out, collect, accumulate, authenticate, disseminate precise information across the organization, and then utilize it across different stages of organization to create custom-made exclusive guest experiences.

Importance of Customer Relationship Management in Hotel Industry

Customer focus and customer service attention is

not a new notion. It is unquestionably a long-standing corporate dynamic. CRM is a progression rather than a revolution. As a result, every company's main goal should be to maximise the value of each client connection. The importance of quality service and customer satisfaction is recognised in India's tourism industry, and modern hotels respect this. According to academics, the modern Indian hotel industry should focus on customer-centric services and marketing communication methods to gain a lasting competitive advantage.

CRM has been acknowledged as a critical technique in the hotel industry. Despite the increasing body of literature demonstrating the value of CRM in the hotel industry, there is a need for more investigation. In the hotel business, a few research works were carried out to explore the influence of CRM and its determinants on different aspects of organisational performance. Therefore, it is required to observe the relationship between aspects of CRM, as well as organisation performance.

Significance of CRM in Hotel Industry

CRM is essential for the modern corporate sector to meet the purpose of business promotion, facilitate the delivery of customer-centric goods and services, and maximise corporate reputation. Customer relations are most important to modern organisations to understand the value, needs, requirements, and behavioural patterns of customers. Due to the surge of globalisation, stiff competition, increased customer turnover, rising client acquisition costs, and increasing consumer expectations, hotels' profitability and competitiveness are heavily reliant on their potential to offer customer service in an efficient and quick manner.

A variety of problems have hampered CRM adoption in the hospitality industry. These include the industry's continuing fragmentation, separate, proprietary, and generally undeveloped IT systems, complexities linked with dealing a perishable commodity supplied through several distribution channels. A systematic adaptation of CRM methods and implementation of CRM technologies will result in quick advancement in the hospitality management sector. In a highly dynamic business set-up, the needs and expectations of each and every customer must be met by the hotel industry. It's essential to comprehend the business performance components that inspire clients to buy from them again and again, as well as to show behavioural loyalty.

Need for CRM in Hotel Industry

CRM is critical to establishing a client-driven company in a five-star hotel. CRM is a critical component in the development of a hotel's customer base and sales capacity. Consumers have innumerable options today, for star hotels targeted customers are more valuable. Thus, the hotel sector cannot survive without them. Star hotels may use CRM to manage all areas of client relations in such a way that they can maximise profits from each customer. Coordination with business operations, strategy, employee and customer acceptance are all important components of a successful CRM strategy.

CRM contributes to higher performance in the hotel business. This will be feasible due to the attributes of CRM, which promotes these essential business success elements viz., the push for enhanced quality of service and technology driven customer satisfaction, and two-way communication. Quality of service evaluation on a constant basis have become a critical component in assuring the success of service. Similarly, the quality of service is the defining factor for an organisation in this cut-throat competition. Customers will be satisfied as long as the service rendered to them is of high quality. Customer satisfaction is a vital functional goal for managers in the hotel industry. In this context, CRM is critical in ensuring that businesses understand their customers' demands and provide customized services. Furthermore, CRM is more crucial than ever for the service business because it is the glue that holds the client and the organisation together. He further opined that in order to make the whole process possible it is important to integrate information technology systems and applications with CRM.

Scope of Customer Relationship Management in Hotel Industry

In the hotel industry, customer relationship management has a wide and considerable influence, greatly increasing both operational efficiency and guest pleasure. The hotel industry may profit greatly from CRM, but there are certain drawbacks as well. For example, the installation process can be costly, time-consuming, and difficult. Hotels have the ability to gather and combine large volumes of client data via various channels and visitor cycles. As a result, CRM presents hotels with the chance to leverage this data to enhance customer satisfaction and retention by strengthening their relationship with clients and the quality of their services.

Let's get a closer look at the wider-scope of customer relationship management as mentioned below:

A. Management of Guest Data:

Storage of Data in Centralised Form: CRM systems

store comprehensive guest profiles, including personal preferences, past stay history, feedback, and special requests, in a centralized database.

Analysis of Data: Analyze guest data to understand preferences and trends, enabling more personalized and targeted services.

B. Personalization of Customer Experience:

Service Customisation: Use CRM data to tailor services to individual guest preferences, such as room type, preferred amenities, and dining choices.

Communication in Personalised Form: Send personalized emails and offers based on guest history and preferences, enhancing the guest experience and building loyalty.

C. Marketing and Sales:

Segmented Campaigns: Segment the guest database to run targeted marketing campaigns and promotions, improving the effectiveness of marketing efforts.

Upselling and Cross-Selling: Identify opportunities for upselling and cross-selling additional services, such as spa treatments, dining options, and room upgrades.

D. Enhancement of Loyalty Programs:

Management of Loyalty Programmes: Manage and track loyalty programs efficiently, rewarding guests based on their stay history and engagement.

Retention of Customer: Use CRM to identify and engage repeat guests with special offers and loyalty benefits, increasing retention rates.

E. Improvement in Customer Feedback System:

Gathering of Feeback: Automate the collection of guest feedback through surveys and reviews, providing valuable insights into guest satisfaction.

Resolving Problems: Track and manage guest

complaints and service recovery actions to ensure timely and satisfactory resolution.

F. **Efficiency in Operations:**

Automation of Taks: Automate routine tasks such as follow-up emails, booking confirmations, and check-in/check-out processes, freeing up staff to focus on more complex tasks.

Allocation of Resources: Use CRM data to optimize resource allocation, such as staffing levels and inventory management, based on guest demand and preferences.

G. **Management of Sales and Revenue:**

Managing Leads: Track and manage sales leads, inquiries, and conversions through the CRM system to streamline the sales process.

Optimizing Revenue: Analyze booking patterns and guest spending behaviors to develop pricing strategies that maximize revenue.

H. **Relationship Managment:**

Engaging Customers: Maintain ongoing communication with guests before, during, and after their stay to build lasting relationships.

Creating Community: Create a sense of community through newsletters, social media engagement, and exclusive member events.

I. **Integrating with Other Systems:**

Unified Integration: Amalgamation of customer relationship management system with other systems of hotel management such as Property Management Systems (PMS), Point of Sale (POS) systems, and bookings for a flow of data that is seamless along with increased efficiency in operations.

Unified Opinion: Providing a amalgamated understanding of customer interactions and transactions across different touchpoints, improving the delivery of service and enhancing coordination.

J. **Reports and Analysis:**

Keeping a Track of Performance: Generating detailed reports to track key performance indicators such as occupancy rates, customer satisfaction scores, and revenue metrics.

Tactical Understandings: Using analytics to gain insights into different tends of market, behaviours of customers, and performance of operations, aiding in strategic decision-making.

Conclusion

Customer relationship management is used widely in the hotel sector, addressing many facets of operations, marketing, guest management, and strategic planning. Hotels can increase revenue and visitor loyalty, optimise operational efficiencies, and improve guest experiences by utilising systems of customer relationship management to their full potential. In order to satisfy changing guest expectations and market circumstances, it is imperative that capabilities of customer relationship management be continually integrated and adapted.

CHAPTER – VI

Implementation of CRM in Business Enterprise

"The single most important thing in sales is the number of very well-organized activities. Hence a good and easy-to-use CRM is a must." – **Greg GutKowski**, *Principal at 3Clicks.*

Introduction

Before a hotel may prudently hold new business chances, it must first recognise the demands of its patrons as a hospitality sector. CRM is a new management tool designed to enhance business and customer relationships. It views the core hotel business clientele as a valuable resource and strategically approaches meeting their needs through enhanced customer service and in-depth customer analysis. This allows hotels to maximise client satisfaction and loyalty, build strong, mutually beneficial relationships over the long term, and maximise customer lifetime value. Hotels require a thorough understanding of their customers in order to please them and build positive relationships with them. This includes learning about their personalities, interests, and how best to give services and goods to them.

As a result, the concept of CRM emphasises the notion that customers are valuable resources. Hotels rationally aim for long-term commercial success, which implies that their success increases with the strength of their client relationships. The hotel industry revolves around its customers. Customer happiness is essential to a business's existence. Customers are prepared to pay more for superior services and expect them to be of a higher calibre. From the standpoint of the client, high-quality service results in enduring relationships that are gauged by cross-selling and re-patronage, as well as referrals from happy clients.

Implementation of CRM

After discussing the procedure and the function of CRM inside the company, it is important to give implementation concerns careful thought. CRM operations depend on data and technology processes and systems, but the returns on investments in these areas are at risk if there is insufficient human contact with these processes and systems. If CRM is implemented correctly, the workforce of the organisation will eventually comprehend the procedure. This indicates that a training program will support the process and guarantee high-quality service delivery.

Fig 7
Theoretical Model of CRM Implementation

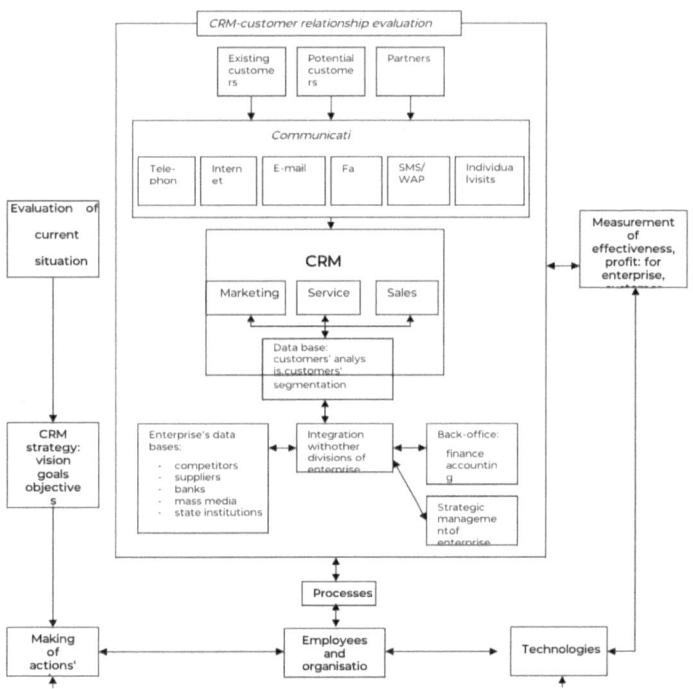

Source: Rūta Urbanskienė, Daiva **Žostautienė,** Virginija Chreptavičienė (2008). The Model of Creation of Customer Relationship Management (CRM) System. Engineering Economics.

Key Components of CRM Implementation

Numerous academics have maintained that before using CRM, an organisation should do a capability audit. There are four key components to CRM implementation that must be met for it to be beneficial.

Organization support

Relationship marketing is seen as a paradigm shift in terms of marketing strategy. There may be a change from mass marketing to individual marketing, as seen by the steady, rapid rise of relationship market approaches, which are similar to one-to-one marketing trends. This school of thought contends that relationship-oriented strategies have gained more traction in the last several years. An organisation needs effective CRM to attract and keep lucrative customers, who might be quite large in number. A more thorough strategy is required for the creation and application of CRM in order to have a successful CRM inside an organisation.

In this regard, the organisation needed to have a rigorous approach and plan as to how to deploy a more complete and integrated CRM. The organisational structure and skills may serve as a metaphor for the connections that exist between the company and its clients. CRM calls for more participation from the whole company, not just the marketing division. This evolution necessitates a cross-functional strategy inside the company. CRM processes necessitate a clear, cohesive, cross-functional strategy. The whole organization's participation and engagement is essential to the effectiveness and efficiency of the CRM.

Organisations must, however, also implement significant organisational and cultural transformation. This means that a management and strategic adjustment is needed for the CRM program. Political project proponents, who typically hold the positions of president, manager, partner, and chairman of the board, are usually involved in a successful CRM implementation. Their primary responsibility is to guarantee that the department or company is able to effectively compete in the complex market. Innovation concept ability, marketing response, and development tendency analysis are critical skills for company executives. Top executives have the ability to ensure CRM implementation and strategic direction. Furthermore, these managers' positions at the top can guarantee changes to the organisational structure, which will allow them to get rid of carriers and use CRM.

Technology Support

Since technology fosters one-to-one relationships, it will improve the application of CRM strategy. CRM in the hotel business has so come to be seen increasingly as a plethora of technologies. It is important to understand that CRM is a business problem rather than a technological one, even if it needs technological tools and capability to help in relationship facilitation. In this regard, CRM has to be supported by technology that enables the organisation to effectively connect people—both customers and employees—with process, people, and business strategy. The system of infrastructure functions according to a domino effect.

CRM is defined as a system that may be constructed via the integration of business operations, technology, and customer service. Automated call centres, customer data warehouses, data mining, customer content, targeted email delivery, and advertising are common instances of how business processes and technical tools are combined. The most popular and often used methods for facilitating the infrastructure needed to deploy CRM are data warehouses and data mining. The term "data warehouse" refers to a location where centralised customer data is stored. However, data mining is the act of examining client data from several angles and condensing it into information that can be utilised for the desired purpose. They play a critical role in identifying the market segment, customer lifetime value, buying habits, contribution margins, and demographics of the customer base. The infrastructure of technology is a mechanism for obtaining and classifying consumer data. So, in order to facilitate one-on-one communication, the organisation needs an efficient technology infrastructure for information access and dissemination. The organization's data mining methodology and technological advancements boost CRM performance. To enhance the CRM, several businesses employ various information technology and data warehousing solutions.

Businesses may target their consumers more successfully by utilising the range of techniques and CRM technologies available. A consistent customer image should be maintained throughout the whole organisation and should be presented across all of the many channels that a client may use to communicate with the business. This is known as good customer relationship management.

Technology makes this possible by collecting data through direct communication and engagement channels. Technology also makes it possible to store data in a way that makes it useful across a variety of channels and for strategic purposes. Since customers' operations don't fit into conventional functional organisations, the two most crucial considerations for deploying CRM systems are process flexibility and data integration.

Employees Support

The most significant role in the creation and use of CRM is played by employees. Employee involvement, which is supported by training and expertise, plays a major role in ensuring a positive customer experience. Employee involvement guarantees customer-focused service. Employees that are driven by service put the needs of the client first, which helps the company create and execute a well-planned CRM. An enthusiastic and dedicated worker made a significant contribution to the company's success.

An employee who is well-trained and skilled will thus have a comprehensive understanding of the company's CRM strategy. plays a crucial function in the implementation procedure at the end. In this regard, it can be claimed that workers are the CRM's blocking building. Although managerial and technological tools are crucial, people also play a significant part in the CRM implementation process. Furthermore, the degree to which employees are aware of the organization's mission has a significant influence on their interactions with customers.

Customer information management

Companies must gather and incorporate pertinent client data into the database in order to use CRM. Companies analyse and use consumer data to better understand and segment their client base. Lastly, implement the study via real-world initiatives that satisfy consumer desire. The database must be filled out with client information in order for CRM to be finished. Any activity related to customer relationship management starts with this. Businesses are able to obtain certain client information from each encounter. It is crucial to maintain an updated client database. Because consumer and market demands are always shifting. Companies that use outdated information will struggle with their marketing campaigns. Companies need to ensure their information intake and flow change with the changing market conditions.

Segmenting and analysing client data is the second phase. Numerous multivariate statistical techniques, including credit scoring, customer profiling, discriminant analysis, cluster analysis, and campaign management analysis, are available for analysing customer data. These techniques make it possible to analyse vast amounts of data and find important links and patterns. Using these techniques, businesses may initially create distinct product offerings or marketing campaigns for various client groups based on the behavioural tendencies of those groups. Companies can also determine the potential earnings that each client can generate for them, allowing them to offer various products or services to various profitable clientele or groups. Additionally, businesses can choose their primary target market by identifying the profitable clients.

Sharing the information is the next step after collecting and analysing the consumer data. CRM facilitates communication between sales, marketing, and customer support by exchanging customer data. By sharing customer information throughout the whole organisation, businesses may transform a customer's connection with one department into a relationship with the entire organisation. The process of gathering, storing, exchanging, and managing customer information inside an organisation is known as customer information management. Customer knowledge management plays a key role in CRM systems as they are built to give businesses a comprehensive understanding of their clientele.

Conclusion

These days, owners and managers are increasingly persuaded to use CRM in their business to increase revenue and profit, the calibre of the goods and services, and the customer satisfaction and retention. By putting into practice a good CRM, the advantages are becoming more apparent, and the Businesses are more eager to use CRM. systems. Even though there are a tonne of advantages for businesses that arise from putting into practice CRM, yet there are several advantages that will have a favourable effect on clients as well.

CHAPTER – VII

Measurement of CRM: Organisational Performance Perspective

"If you make a sale, you can make a living. If you make an investment of time and good service in a customer, you can make a fortune." – **Jim Rohn**, *Author and Motivational Speaker.*

Introduction

The goal of management objectives and strategies is to improve organisational performance. According to major management theories, such as all contingency theories, include organisational performance as a key dependent variable in their conceptual reasoning. Performance is defined as the sum of all the organization's work processes and activities. It refers to an organization's ability to convert inputs into outputs and includes the actual output or results as compared to its intended outputs. Organizational performance comprises three distinct areas of business outcomes: financial performance, product market performance, and shareholder return, however it is also contending that firm performance is the firm's ability to succeed. Several authors have identified a number of characteristics that are thought to be crucial to the effectiveness of performance measurement. In management research, firm performance is an important construct that is usually utilised as a dependent variable. In numerous domains, it is one of the most widely utilised constructs as the last dependent variable. It is vital to establish and select relevant performance measures and targets. The majority of these indicators fall into one of four categories: profitability, quality, productivity, and growth, and customer satisfaction. For years, financial performance evaluation was viewed as the only, proper, and valid technique of analysing an organization's effectiveness and efficiency. Performance evaluation can be divided into seven categories namely effectiveness, productivity, quality, customer satisfaction, efficiency, innovation, and financial stability.

CRM Dimensions and Organisational Performance

Various techniques of conceptualising and measuring performance have been used in studies on company performance. Performance is a multi-dimensional phenomenon that cannot be effectively expressed in a single performance item. This argument proposes that a composite measure of performance, rather than a single qualitative or accounting-related performance indicator, would more effectively reflect a firm's improvements. As a result, this study used the balanced scorecard (BSC) approach to measure organisational performance, because BSC includes not only financial measures (measures based on financial metrics) but also three non-financial measures: customers (measures concerned with what matters to customers); internal process (measures related to critical internal processes in which the organisation must excel to implement strategy); and learning and growth. In industrial, service industries, and non-profit organisations, the BSC approach has been widely employed. Business journalists have hailed the concept as a game-changer in terms of performance assessment and reporting. It also translates mission and strategy into objectives and measurable terms from the financial, customer, internal business process, and learning and growth perspectives by striking a balance between short- and long-term goals. Financial numbers alone cannot provide a complete knowledge of CRM's influence and results; consequently, the overall performance viewpoint should be included in CRM results evaluation.

As a result, utilising BSC to assess the influence of CRM on organisational performance is crucial, as it is a good tool for assessing an organization's overall performance. To summarise, the BSC approach assesses business performance using both financial and non-financial metrics and provides businesses with a comprehensive picture of their operations and performance. Because hotels consist of many distinct activities with diverse cost structures, such as food (restaurant), housekeeping, point-of-sale (front office), and receiver (storeroom), the use of BSC to measure hotel performance has been appropriated here. Because of the wide range of activities, financial measures alone are insufficient. Organizations also strive to improve client interactions with CRM. Hence, any measure of success must include the viewpoint of the customers. So, this study employs the BSC idea as a framework for evaluating organisational performance in the service sector to better understand the impact of CRM characteristics on organisational performance.

Fig 8
Conceptual Model of the influence of CRM Dimensions on Hotel Performance

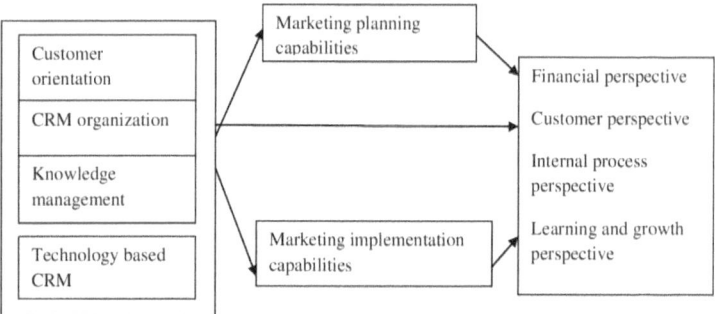

Source: Mohammed, A.A., & Rashid, B.B. (2012).

Solid CRM process measure that identifies three critical stages: commencement, maintenance, and termination. The deployment of CRM processes has a relatively good relationship with both perceptual and objective firm performance. Different dimensions of organisational performance (i.e., internal process, growth, and learning, and financial and customer) and CRM dimensions (i.e., technology-based CRM, knowledge management, customer orientation, and CRM organisation) relate to each other in hotels. All the dimensions of CRM have a good and significant impact on hotel performance (technology-based CRM, knowledge management, customer orientation, and CRM organization).

Customer relationships dimensions have a considerable positive impact on hotel performance. Furthermore, the the CRM aspects and organisational performance have a favourable relationship. From particular research it was discovered that information technology utilisation has a significant impact on CRM success, as well as customer orientation, organisational competency, and customer knowledge management.

There is a link between CRM success and organisational performance, with the following elements influencing CRM success: customer orientation, organisational capability, information technology, and customer knowledge management.

It also confirmed through research that the role of Information Technology reliability (IT) as a factor potentially strengthening CRM influence on organisational performance and to determine whether IT reliability is an important factor shaping CRM ability to generate value for an organisation. IT solutions support CRM, and that with this assistance, the management style has a beneficial impact on organisational performance.

The CRM's current strategy as a business management tool which is to build channels and techniques to manage customer-centered information in order to improve organisational performance and to achieve better business results. A study was conducted to confirm the initial assumptions regarding the projected positive impact of using the technology solution CRM on company outcomes. A detailed review of numerous ideas that identify both the installation and use of CRM, as well as the factors that identify the results or measurements of organisational performance. Expectations about CRM's impact on company performance may be compatible with the successful and proven results in organisations that have implemented and are utilising CRM internally.

Conclusion

Since meeting the requirements of consumers is an organization's main objective and will improve profit, this suggests that company operations would be pointless without clients. CRM is the key to success regardless of the type of client—internal or external, consumers or enterprises, connecting digitally or in person from across the world or across town. Since attracting and keeping consumers is the goal of any organisation, CRM practices are essential. It is the most effective tool available to any corporate organisation that prioritises services above just products. In every area of their business, every organisation has to stress how crucial CRM is to maintaining their goodwill.

Thus, businesses make every effort to both keep and win over new clients. Establishing routes and methods for managing customer centre information is one of the strategies of customer relationship management as a business management tool. This will enhance organisational performance and lead to improved business outcomes. Consequently, building strong client connections enables a company to expand its line of business and contend with fierce rivalry.

CHAPTER – VIII

Measurement of CRM: Customers' Benefit Perspective

"Yes, CRM is all about Customer Relationship Management ... but it is also about prospect relationships." — **Bobby Darnell**

Introduction

CRM is a strategy that combines technology, business, and people to better understand customer demands and increase customer satisfaction. Consumers are the essential component that allows every business or corporation to expand. Thus, one of the key strategies that managers and businesses may use to improve customer happiness and loyalty is the use of CRM applications. In addition, there are other advantages that clients will experience following CRM implementation. These advantages will make it easier for clients to enjoy and be satisfied with the businesses that use CRM facilities to sell their goods and services.

Despite the fact that CRM has a significant influence on businesses and organisations, there are a number of advantages and benefits that also directly benefit customers, increasing customer happiness and retention. An essential component of management is evaluating and determining the advantages of CRM. These advantages will assist businesses in determining how to improve client relationships more effectively, which will ultimately result in business profits.

Indicators of CRM Measurement: Customer Perspective

The following dimensions are the indicators of measurement of customer relationship management from a customer's perspective.

Enhancement of Customer Service

Customer service is the exchange of information between a client and the business, usually by standard means like email or phone. Customers will frequently have requests or concerns that they would like addressed. CRM services give a company the capacity to generate, distribute, and oversee client requests. One CRM feature that businesses and organisations may use is Call Centre software, which facilitates the connection between a client and the manager or other individual who can help them with their current issue. Acknowledging and utilising this kind of service may assist businesses in enhancing customer service by increasing efficiency and reducing expenses, as well as improving client understanding. Some of the CRM applications' capabilities that can affect the quality of customer service include personalised services, the ability to recognise and reward profitable customers, the creation and scheduling of appointments with customers, the customisation of marketing campaigns and the sending of messages to specific customers, multi-channel communication, and increased responsiveness to customer needs. A company that provides excellent customer service will meet its clients' requirements and maintain its financial competitiveness. Increasing the calibre of customer service is one of the major benefits of CRM implementation in any business.

Enhanced Personalized Service

Personalised services are those that involve interacting with, marketing to, and taking care of people by offering a unique and noteworthy personal experience. The focus is on the individual and customisation. Understanding a customer's wants and requirements by asking questions, listening to their responses, and seeing them in action is known as one-to-one service. Thus, one-on-one or personalised customer service helps businesses learn more about their clients and show them that they value their business. It also helps businesses understand the preferences, needs, and desires of their clients.

Receptive to Needs & Wants of Customer

CRM is a method to learn more about customers' wants and requirements in order to establish strong connections with them. It is not only an application of technology. Giving clients what they want, no more, no less, is being attentive to their needs. CRM is an effective tool that businesses may use to concentrate more on being responsive to their customers. CRM involves collecting data on clients in order to identify more effective methods to meet their demands. Take the connection to the next level by concentrating on the wants and expectations of the consumer.

It demonstrates that businesses can comprehend the demands and circumstances of their clients. Every client has the right to expect businesses to anticipate what would benefit them by identifying and meeting their unmet needs and wants. It is then necessary to transform these unidentified needs and wants into new goods and services. CRM is an important tool that will assist businesses in understanding and meeting the demands of their clients and in taking accountability for those needs.

Categorization of Customer

The practice of classifying objects or items into groups based on shared qualities is known as segmentation. Despite the fact that these qualities can be one or many. It may be characterised as a popularity subdivide based on well-established discriminators. CRM uses segmentation to group clients based on shared characteristics, such industry. There are other methods for categorising and segmenting data, but for the sake of this study, we only want to concentrate on the advantages of segmentation for consumers. In consumer markets, demographics, psychographics, and behavioural traits like benefits requirements or loyalty status are three common categories of segmentation factors. A company's focus was directed on aligning marketing initiatives and product offerings with customer demands through the use of segmentation or target marketing. To identify client wants and preferences, businesses must characterise tinier and more discrete groupings. As a result, clients may be divided into groups according to factors like age, gender, and demographics. CRM will make it possible to segment clients according to their demands through this. It will assist businesses in grouping their clientele into comparable categories based on their needs. CRM software will help businesses with the segmentation process.

Enhancement of Market Customization

Customised marketing refers to how a business or organisation adjusts and modifies its offerings in order to provide each client with a special set of goods or services. The organisation uses customisation to make sure that the demands and requirements of the customers are satisfied. Businesses might spend money gathering consumer data and then use that data to tailor their products as much as possible to meet the needs of their target market. Additionally, consumer communications may be tailored to improve a particular customer's experience with a product or service. CRM offers clients the benefit of customised products and services due to its capacity to customise the latter.

Amalgamation of Multiple Channels

Today's customers have a wider variety of channels to choose from, therefore a successful CRM must handle client relationships more effectively in a multichannel setting. Since a large portion of customer knowledge is acquired in this channel environment, technology, customer potential, and competitive factors are increasingly persuading local businesses and organisations to support customer service activities from certain delivery channels. As it transforms the outcomes of value-creation processes and corporate strategy into customer communications that add value, multichannel integration development bears a significant duty in CRM. The acquisition, extension, and retention stages of CRM may all be maintained with multi-channel integration. When merchants adopt a transactional marketing strategy and are solely focused on achieving successful customer outcomes, multi-channel integration works well. As a result, even if only one or two of the three goals are met, multi-channel integration is still beneficial when implementing the CRM approach.

Saving Time

A faster time to market is important for businesses trying to gain a competitive advantage. Customers must also receive prompt responses from the business during the sales process so they don't have to waste time on the purchasing or product delivery processes. CRM skills may help businesses respond to consumers by streamlining the development and deployment cycle. CRM solutions allow IT to be more responsive to business demands by bringing in capabilities and upgrades faster and at a reduced cost. Reducing the amount of paper used at work or while interacting with clients is one of the helpful advantages of adopting a CRM system. With a CRM solution, all operations that were performed using forms and paperwork may be virtualised and automated. In addition to saving time and money on paper costs, this procedure also helps a business become more ecologically conscious in the eyes of its clientele.

Enhancement of Customer Knowledge

One of the reasons a company installs CRM systems is to monitor client behaviour in relation to their demands and preferences. Businesses may use this information to create and develop improved goods and services. Given the constant evolution of consumer knowledge, CRM software aid organisations in better understanding their clientele by examining their purchasing patterns across various channels. CRM systems provide businesses a competitive edge in enhancing the way they gather consumer data so they can better tailor their products and services to the demands of their clients. Customers can also profit from customer knowledge since it makes it possible for the business to respond to their demands based on their purchase patterns and the appropriate services. Customer knowledge may therefore be used to determine the consumers' preferences and customise the items.

Conclusion

New technologies impact businesses by quickening the flow of information and knowledge through them. These days, owners and managers are progressively coming around to the idea that implementing CRM will increase their company's income and profit, as well as the quality of their goods and services, client retention, and satisfaction. Benefits from a successful CRM implementation are becoming apparent, and businesses are becoming more interested in utilising CRM systems. While using CRM may provide several benefits for businesses, there are also perks that will positively affect customers.

It goes without saying that increasing and improving these advantages will boost client retention and satisfaction. Therefore, ensuring client satisfaction increases sales and profits for the company. Therefore, it is crucial for each company's strategist and policy makers to comprehend and enhance CRM's benefits from the perspective of the consumer, since this can ultimately result in customer happiness.

CHAPTER- IX

Revolution in Hotel CRM: Use of Artificial Intelligence

"One customer well taken care of could be more valuable than $10,000 worth of advertising." – **Jim Rohn**

Introduction

The hotel sector is faced with previously unheard-of opportunities and problems in the modern, fast-paced digital environment. Hotels need to change to remain competitive as guest expectations rise. Customer relationship management (CRM) systems driven by artificial intelligence (AI) are among the most promising alternatives available today. These cutting-edge tools are revolutionising the way hotels engage with their patrons, run their businesses, and foster company expansion.

This trend represents a significant turning point for hotels. Competitors are starting to use AI-powered CRM, and those that don't adjust risk being left behind. With the competitive hospitality industry, hotels are finding it more and more important to be able to handle large volumes of visitor data, generate actionable insights, and deliver personalised experiences at scale. These are skills that AI-enhanced CRM systems give hotels. This means that hotels have a lot of opportunities:

Artificial Intelligence and its implementation in Customer Relationship Management

Personalised Marketing: Artificial Intelligence can develop focused marketing efforts by examining visitor preferences, booking patterns, and behaviour. Conversion rates and visitor loyalty may both be greatly increased with this level of personalisation.

Dynamic Pricing: Artificial Intelligence algorithms can maximise hotel income by optimising room prices in real-time depending on demand, rival pricing, and other variables.

Predictive analytics: Artificial Intelligence can estimate occupancy rates by evaluating past data, which helps hotels more effectively manage workforce and inventory.

Automated Upselling: Using visitor profiles and preferences, Artificial Intelligence may find chances to suggest upgrades or other services.

Artificial Intelligence in Personalization and Improved Guest Experience

Tailored Recommendations: It may provide recommendations for services, meals, or activities based on a visitor's tastes and historical usage.

Customised Room Settings: Artificial Intelligence driven systems are able to recognise a visitor's preferences regarding lighting, temperature, and even the contents of the minibar, and will make the necessary adjustments for their next visit.

Personalised Communication: It can increase engagement by customising the content, tone, and timing of communications to each visitor's preferences.

Artificial Intelligence in Enhancing Customer Service

24/7 Virtual Concierge: Artificial Intelligence driven chatbots can respond to visitor enquiries immediately, covering routine queries and freeing up people to address more complicated problems.

Effective Query Routing: It can determine the type of question a visitor is asking and direct them to the right department or employee, speeding up the response time.

Predictive Problem-Solving: It can predict typical problems and proactively provide answers by examining patterns in visitor enquiries. This increases visitor happiness.

Artificial Intelligence in Increasing Operational Efficiency

Streamlined Check-in/Check-out: It can automate a number of procedures related to check-in and check-out, cutting down on wait times and enhancing visitor satisfaction.

Effective Cleaning: It is capable of optimising cleaning schedules according to visitor preferences, room occupancy, and personnel availability.

Automated Maintenance: Artificial Intelligence systems are able to anticipate when equipment needs to be maintained, eliminating malfunctions and guaranteeing that rooms are always available for guests.

Staff Training: It can provide staff members instantaneous direction, enabling them to manage visitor encounters more skilfully.

Artificial Intelligence's Growing Importance in

Readiness of Data

Data cleaning: It can verifiy that all guest information is correct, current, and devoid of mistakes or duplication.

Data Integration: It can construct a thorough visitor profile by merging data from several touchpoints, including as bookings, on-property interactions, and post-stay surveys, to break down data silos.

Data Compliance: It can abide with laws like GDPR and win over guests' trust, put in place strong data protection procedures.

Data Governance: It can guarantee the ethical application of AI, clearly define regulations for data collection, utilisation, and storage.

Artificial Intelligence in Managing Concerns of Trust and Security

Data protection: It can safeguard sensitive visitor information by using CRM providers with robust security protocols.

Transparency: It can explain to visitors how their data is being utilised to improve their stay.

Opt- Out Options: It can provide visitors simple ways to choose not to participate in interactions or data collecting.

Human Oversight: It can put in place mechanisms that allow employees to assess suggestions to make sure they are accurate and suitable.

Artificial Intelligence and its Challenges

Cost of Implementation: AI technology can be costly to purchase, particularly for smaller hotels.

Staff Education: To properly collaborate with AI systems, staff members must get education.

Guest Acceptance: It's important to take a balanced approach because certain visitors could find AI-driven interactions unpleasant.

Data Quality: Both the volume and quality of the accessible data determine how effective AI systems are.

Ethical Considerations: Hotels need to carefully consider the ethical ramifications of using AI, particularly with relation to visitor privacy and data usage.

Industries that are resistant to adopting new technical innovations in the twenty-first century are likely to regress in their development. Companies all throughout the world have come to understand how crucial it is to integrate modern digital technologies in order to sustain development and income. In the modern hotel sector, where comfort-defining innovations are implemented most quickly, the entire system has become more complex via the adoption of several cutting-edge techniques for delivering excellent customer service.

Important Statistics on the Use of Artificial Intelligence in Hotels

With a startling compound annual growth rate of 60%, the AI in hospitality industry, which was valued at USD 90 million in 2022, is predicted to reach an astounding USD 8,120 million by 2033. Hotels that use AI-powered revenue management systems have seen a rise in total income of 10%, while AI-assisted automated check-in kiosks have slashed customer wait times by around 30%. Additionally, with the use of artificial intelligence, 68% of hotel websites worldwide already provide automated online services. These figures demonstrate how AI is changing the industry's approach to the visitor experience.

The Notion Behind Creating Intelligent Hotels

The approach that many contemporary hospitality leaders and service partners envision is having an intelligent hotel that goes above and beyond what guests anticipate. The hotel sector is adopting AI services to improve visitor experiences by using AI-driven solutions for individualised support and effective operations. Hotels are clever because of a few key components. Some of which are:
- Concierge Robots
- Digital Assistance
- Voice-Activated Services
- Travel Experience Enhancers
- Automatic Data Processing

Fig.9 - Humanoid Robots

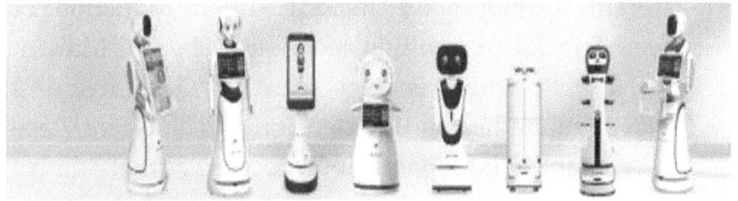

Source: Alpha Robotics Co. Ltd (www.alpharobotics.com)

Fig.- 10 Concierge Robot   Fig.-11 Voice Activated Service

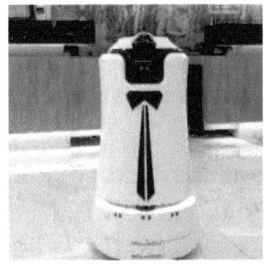 

Source: Remora Networks Solutions **Source:** orangemantra (www.remora-solutions.com) (ww w.organgemantra.com)

The Rise of Intelligent Hotels in India and World Over

The next frontier for leaders and service providers in India's hospitality industry is intelligent hotels. To improve the visitor experience, these establishments make advantage of AI-powered care support services. Customers now have greater control over how they engage with the service they receive and feel comfortable thanks to these fresh and inventive AI-driven changes in the hospitality industry. AI is being used by hotel chains for everyday operations automation and revenue management. As of right now, India is already going through this change, with numerous hotel chains—including the Sheraton, ITC Welcom, Taj, and Oberoi groups—benefiting from technology and artificial intelligence in areas like cooking, reservations, booking, billing, and comfort for overall guest satisfaction.

Recent developments include the introduction of AI-powered facial recognition technology by the Marriot group of hotels, which enables seamless check-ins; and the Park Inn by Radission IP Extension, which offers voice assistance enabled intelligent hotel rooms, virtual control over lighting fixtures and TVs, and automated service requests. An intriguing revelation indicated that the integration of artificial intelligence (AI) into operational systems in the hotel sector in India is expected to boost revenue by 15.2% by 2025.

International Chain of Hotels Across the World Using AI driven CRM Technology

Four Seasons: Four Seasons is a luxury hotel chain that has long been known for its exceptional customer service. The chain has implemented a number of initiatives to improve guest satisfaction, including the Four Seasons App, which allows guests to customize their stay, order room service, and make requests directly from their mobile device.

The Ritz-Carlton: The Ritz-Carlton has a strong focus on personalized service and creating a memorable experience for guests. The chain has implemented a number of initiatives to improve guest satisfaction, including the creation of a "mystery shopper" program to ensure that staff are delivering exceptional service at all times.

Marriott International: Marriott International has implemented AI-powered chatbots to enhance the guest experience and improve customer service. The chatbots use natural language processing (NLP) to provide guests with instant responses to their queries and requests, enabling them to access information and services quickly and easily.

Hilton Hotels & Resorts: Hilton Hotels & Resorts has implemented an AI-powered concierge service that uses machine learning to provide personalized recommendations and assistance to guests. The concierge service can suggest local restaurants, attractions, and activities based on the guest's preferences and previous behavior.

InterContinental Hotels Group (IHG): IHG has implemented AI-powered voice assistants in its hotel rooms to provide guests with personalized services and recommendations. The voice assistants can control room temperature, lighting, and TV, as well as provide information about hotel services and local attractions.

A Look to the Future

The hotel business stands to benefit greatly from the use of Artificial Intelligence into CRM systems. Hotels may improve visitor experiences, expedite processes, and obtain a competitive edge in a market that is becoming more and more digital by utilising AI-powered CRM. But using AI-powered CRM successfully calls for more than just putting new technologies into place. Hotels need to focus on becoming data ready, handle issues with security and trust, and properly handle the adoption hurdles of Artificial Intelligence.

Future predictions indicate that AI-powered CRM will become more and more important to the hotel sector. The hotel industry is changing, and those that use this technology carefully and strategically will be in a good position to prosper. The message is obvious for hotels thinking about making the switch to AI-powered CRM: artificial intelligence is driving the hospitality industry of the future. Hotels can make sure they are ready to satisfy the evolving expectations of tomorrow's visitors by taking the necessary preparations today for an AI-driven future.

Apart from the possibility of partnering with a soft brand or an internationally recognised brand partner, what could AI entail for hotel owners? AI may continue to focus the market into residences with lots of facilities and those with little, along with these domestic and worldwide alliances with businesses in related sectors. Properties in the middle—those with modest or nonexistent amenities—are more likely to do away with them. Meal delivery and on-demand health apps will render mediocre amenities or those with minimal usage practically obsolete, just as ride-service apps have made hotels that are not close to an event more accessible and appealing.

More robotics (for physical jobs) and chatbots (for non-physical tasks) are already being able to do duties that were previously handled by people thanks to the technological and artificial intelligence revolution. Since manpower accounts for around 45% of hotel operating costs, there is undoubtedly a desire to replace labour with technology. Considerable advances in machine intelligence have made it feasible for robots to begin replacing humans in some situations. Machines will become more and more helpful in hotels as a result of technological advancements and the capacity to develop with large databases.

It goes without saying that owners will want to boost their investments in security, preventive maintenance, and energy efficiency. They may even wish to replace some elements of housekeeping and food service with robots. Owners will try to replace labour expenses with lower labour costs and operational costs with depreciation expenditure. In general, visitors to more upscale establishments will want more face-to-face interaction, which supports the theory that properties and capital investments will either skew towards the upper end of the spectrum or entirely self-service.

Conclusion

Nearly, if not all, hotel departments and functions will become beneficiaries of increasing technological efficiencies and the AI revolution. Artificial Intelligence (AI) and machine learning have the potential to revolutionise the hotel industry by enhancing visitor loyalty, optimising experiences, and providing suggestions. Hotels will also be able to find insights and make the most of them with the aid of recommendation engines and sophisticated analytics. Most significantly, though, is that robots could actually appear. The introduction of the Amazon Astro, which is essentially Alexa on wheels, may allow robots to enter the market for personal butlers, providing upscale assistance with customised care. Think about the benefits of having a robot handle physical labour-intensive jobs like picking up and dropping off luggage, moving materials, and making deliveries. Tasks including bartending, housekeeping, and logistics are being begun by robots at hotels. This means more machines and fewer employees will run hotel businesses.

CHAPTER – X

Reliazing the Benefits of Crm

"Yes, CRM is all about Customer Relationship Management... but it is also about Prospect Relationships as well." – **Bobby Darnell**, *Time for Dervin – Living Large In Geiggityville.*

Introduction

One of the standard instruments in the enterprise's toolbox is CRM. Because of how commonplace it has become; firms frequently don't even consider if they need it or what it may do for them. When it comes to witnessing a real increase in income following its implementation, CRM adoption turns out to be a crucial component. While they may not be perfect in every aspect, at least they are headed in the right direction. CRM software is an effective tool for cutting expenses-related inefficiencies in your company. In addition to increasing sales team productivity and enabling them to contact more clients with more pertinent content, it may lower your customer acquisition expenses in a number of ways.

A comprehensive view of your clients and customer connections is one of the most potent advantages that

CRM software provides. This covers their requirements, inclinations, and purchasing habits. Knowing your consumers' demands better makes it easier to, among other things, upsell or cross-sell to them. CRM is a comprehensive system that manages the communication between companies and their customers. It helps firms communicate with customers, understand their needs, and win their support by collecting, organising, and analysing information.

Benefits of Customer Relationship Management

There are two types of benefits that come with CRM: strategic benefits and operational benefits.

Operational Benefits

A successful marketing plan CRM has the potential to increase marketing effectiveness by providing better customer service and by focussing more intently on target consumers. Large volumes of customer data are the foundation of CRM systems; businesses that have mastered this data may further analyse it to give precise direction for marketing strategies with well-defined objectives by analysing consumer attributes, buying patterns, and value orientation. Firstly, comprehensive customer profiles may assist businesses in identifying prospective markets and creating offerings that are appropriate for them. Second, assist the businesses in monitoring the success of their marketing campaigns and offer suggestions and adjustments for future planning.

Companies can begin concentrating on finding new clients and growing their market once they have successfully retained their current clientele. Businesses may find new prospects and grow their customer base more easily the more information they have about their current clientele. By using CRM systems to understand and analyse consumer demands, businesses may develop new services and products that will successfully draw in new clients and expand into untapped markets, giving them an advantage over rivals. A business can identify the clients it does not wish to serve by using customer data analysis and profiling. Businesses may determine which of their clients are successful or unprofitable and, by comprehending client requirements, more precisely determine the demands of their clients by putting CRM into practice.

Services and Customer Service Support

CRM facilitates the gathering and analysis of client data by businesses. Companies can use it to monitor feedback and reactions from customer service in the interim. The process of developing new products and services can be enhanced by this data. The CRM system will log the relevant data from each interaction with the customer. CRM system analysis allows businesses to understand the various demands of their customers. As a result, they can provide a more individualised approach and produce better goods and services. It is possible to prepare these upgrades before clients ask for them.

Proactive customer service and support may effectively and successfully address client demands and problems. Ultimately, businesses are able to get further business in the future. Businesses may quickly ascertain what services or goods consumers desire by gathering customer data or feedback using CRM systems. Businesses will eventually be able to enhance their offerings without incurring additional expenses for specialised market research.

Increase Sales Efficiency

All of the company's current data, including deals, products, competition information, and so on, is kept in the CRM system's central database for salesforce access. Additionally, the system records the sales process of the customer. The contact details and sales history of every client are visible to the staff member with system access. The technology will compile all of the data and assist the business in creating targeted advertising campaigns. Additionally, the instruments of email, internet connection, etc. significantly increase salesforce productivity. Sales personnel inside the organisation are therefore tremendously empowered by salesforce automation.

Knowing which customers are lucrative and which may become profitable in the future allows businesses to identify prospective profitable clients. This is crucial since identifying and concentrating on the clients who have the greatest potential for profit is essential to a successful firm. Businesses may divide consumer values into many levels and completely comprehend the needs of each level by analysing various customer data.

As a result, by concentrating on the most lucrative clients and handling the unproductive ones more economically, the business may increase profitability. Customer retention will rise as a result of CRM systems' ability to improve the effectiveness of business-customer relationships. The current clientele will continue to purchase more often. Because they are typically more receptive, current consumers will typically result in lower sales expenses.

Cross-selling opportunities are also increased by using CRM systems. Cross-selling is the practice of recommending related but supplementary items to current clients. It enables the company to advertise related items that the client might not be aware of or present a free gift that the client could find irresistible and purchase on the spur of the moment. The CRM system will categorise and evaluate the current client data. The business can identify a range of demands among current clients and choose target clients for cross-selling. Therefore, better services or goods are provided to clients by more accurately and more effectively broadening the reach of customer buying. As a result, steer clear of cross-selling blindness and increase its effectiveness.

The advantage of CRM on corporate processes also increases sales efficiency. By enabling real-time information exchange amongst several staff members, CRM implementation enhances telesales, field sales, and sales management. Through the CRM system, staff members may work together and exchange client information. It will assist the business in becoming more effective at identifying customers and resolving their problems. Updates to account information in real time enhance territory management. By identifying, sharing, and using the success and knowledge of your top performers, you can enhance the performance of your whole sales team. Focussing on expanding the top accounts also results in a higher income per call.

Improve Work Efficiency

CRM may improve customer service response efficiency. Businesses may access and update customer information in real time using several CRM system information routes. Retrieving customer information takes much less time. Businesses are able to recognise consumers right away, comprehend their wants quickly, and respond to their demands promptly. to satisfy consumers and leave a positive impression on them about service. The effectiveness of internal communication is also increased when information is shared and transferred using CRM systems.

The CRM system may be used by several departments to share information. As a result, there is a lot of information exchange in the CRM system; staff members don't have to seek other departments for information when they need it. With such excellent communication in the interim, businesses are able to promptly allocate capable response personnel to individual clients. In fact, assigning the appropriate personnel may also help the business reduce its burden.

Strategic Benefits
Customer Segmentation

The goal of customer segmentation is to group consumers into groups based on shared or comparable information. Businesses may offer individualised service to consumers in the same category by using categorisation. One of the most crucial pieces of CRM material is customer segmentation. In the process of deploying CRM, it assists businesses in allocating service resources sensibly and developing the appropriate service plan.

Customer Value

Increasing product quality, innovating new products, and adjusting internal resources inside the company are insufficient to give it a competitive edge. Creating greater consumer value is the secret to gaining an edge over competitors. The source of competitive advantage is from an intuitive knowledge of consumers, who are more likely to buy and repurchase goods and services that they perceive to be higher-value and lower-cost. Businesses may now get a competitive edge by combining their different advantage resources to create goods and services that are more valuable to customers than those of competitors.

Customer Satisfaction

Improving customer happiness and service quality is the goal of CRM deployment. Customer satisfaction in a CRM system is an assessment index of how customers feel about the company's goods and services, both mentally and psychologically. The interaction link between corporate behaviour and consumer behaviour is shown by this intermediate variable. Scholars have suggested since the 1990s that a company's profit stems from its high customer satisfaction rate. They looked into factors including customer happiness, repeat business, and the impact of word-of-mouth on client loyalty. They believe that through a succession of transfers and careful analysis, consumer happiness affects the enterprise's final sales. As a result, customer satisfaction research plays a significant role in CRM theory and is highly valuable.

Customer Loyalty and Customer Retention

Enhanced customer satisfaction has the potential to foster brand loyalty for the product or business. Loyal consumers are more likely to make repeat purchases, refer business to others, and lessen price sensitivity. If consumers behave in this way, businesses may improve customer loyalty and keep customers. Customer satisfaction rises as a result of increased customer value. client happiness leads to client loyalty. Customer loyalty, on the other hand, is mostly fuelled by customer value. Even a tiny gain in client retention can have a significant positive impact on earnings.

Businesses should continue to foster positive relationships with their current clientele while also pursuing new business through a variety of marketing strategies and ultimately turning those prospects into devoted patrons. Competitive advantage has an impact on an organization's short- and long-term business performance. Customer loyalty and satisfaction may be used as indicators of an enterprise's long-term commercial success. This is due to the fact that happy and devoted consumers are more likely to make repeat purchases, promote the business brand positively, and be willing to pay a higher price for goods or services. Market share and profit are typically used to gauge a company's short-term performance. The value that businesses provide for their clients is ultimately what gives them a competitive edge.

Benefits of implementing CRM in Hotel Industry

A CRM system enables hotels to better understand their patrons' demands and build stronger relationships with them. Hotels may eventually be able to compete more successfully in the market. Numerous advantages of using CRM are evident from the examination of both hotels. These advantages fall into two categories: strategic and operational. From an operational standpoint, a CRM system may assist hotels in improving services and products, enhancing sales, and devising efficient marketing tactics. In both instances, they divided their clientele into groups, devised services and amenities for their hotels based on the demands of these groups, and found several ways to upsell.

Additionally, the system can increase operational effectiveness. Each department and chain hotel has the ability to work together and exchange information. The internal procedures are easy to utilise and have been drastically trimmed. From a strategic advantages perspective, hotels may use CRM system to analyse client data and information thoroughly. Consequently, hotels will be able to comprehend and know more about the characteristics of various target groups, customer satisfaction, and customer value distribution. In order to keep guests, hotels will be able to offer higher-quality, more individualised service. Because of those individualised, high-quality services, they were able to satisfy their customers in both situations and earned excellent feedback. Therefore, by consistently enhancing customer-focused services and marketing tactics, hotels may achieve customer happiness, which in turn fosters client loyalty and retention.

Conclusion

Customer relationship management (CRM) has several advantages for firms. These advantages include higher customer satisfaction, higher customer retention, greater communication, more cost-effective sales procedures, and more effective marketing initiatives. CRM adoption may present some difficulties, nevertheless, such as high implementation costs, complicated technology, reluctance to change, worries about data protection, and an excessive dependence on technology. Businesses should develop a detailed implementation strategy, offer assistance and training to employees, guarantee data security and privacy, and periodically review and modify the CRM system in order to overcome these obstacles. Businesses may minimise the negative effects of CRM while optimising its advantages by using these measures.

CHAPTER - XI

Establishing the Priorities for Effective CRM

"Always remember you are there to help your potential customers and to make their lives better. Not the other way around." – David Ferguson, Managing Director at Babel Academy of English.

Introduction

Customer Relationship Management is important for hotels. There are a number of variables that influence customer relationship management in hotels and the differentiation in terms of value proposition from the competitors and homogeneity of hotel product are to name a few and then the market conditions in the modern era too. The necessity of adopting CRM has been emphasized by the globalization and competitive environment it is associate with at the same time there are some contexts, for example the advancement in technology, have supported the need to implement CRM in organisations.

As a matter of fact, there are some environmental factors too that have made CRM as an important and necessary tool that is practically viable to use. One of the most highly sensitive industries happens to be the hotel industry in terms of storing and sharing of information of customers as well as the employees. Information about the customers is so very critical in the CRM process. Further, the information that can be retrieved any time at a given situation does impact significantly on the guests and the hotel organisations alike. However, from the perspective of the customer, easy access to a wealth of information via user-generated content has posed various challenges to hotels. Customer can make more informed decisions as they have an uninterrupted access to the information. As a result, they can take the final call as to when and where they can switch over to the next convenient and desirable option. Due to this phenomena, now-a-days, hotels experience a high attrition rate of customers with rising costs in acquiring new customers. Thus, in this regard, CRM has been suggested as a way to counteract the negative consequences of such a situation.

In today's ever demanding and highly competitive environment, the hotel managers are encountering the toughest task of offering and maintaining customer satisfaction. This has been an important agenda of discussion even for the service providers and the hotel professionals about the rise in demand for products and services of high quality to sustain in the tourism business. It is to be noted that customer satisfaction in key and will continue to be the focus of managers as it is the vital indicator for setting organizational objectives and also a strategic tool to enhance customer relationships in an organization. Hence, effective and meaningful interactions with the customers will enable them to become more inclined and committed for repeat purchase which in turn will help the organization to improve upon the retention rate. Further, a correlation between satisfaction levels of customers and their chances of coming back to the same hotel clearly depends upon the long-term mutually beneficial relationship between the hotel and its prospective customers. More and more hotel organisations are making a conscious effort to invest in order to enhance the quality of services and perceived value for customers that may result in their increased satisfaction and loyalty. The quality of services rendered by the hotel will have a positive influence on the customer's behaviour and create positive word-of-mouth (WOM) and an increased rate of repeat guests.

Priorities for an Effective CRM Implementation

The objective of CRM is to provide a long-standing mutually beneficial connection with the firm and the clients. Different organization derive varying levels of benefits depending upon their commitment and strategies to implement CRM. In the same vein it is hypothesized that customer relationship management does create a whole lot of information about the customers and benefits the organization as a whole. The basic characteristics of service-sector organisations is production and consumption for which it becomes increasingly important for them to develop and maintain an effective relationship with their customers. In this context, customer relationship management is pertinent to the hotel business only if it is applied in an effective manner because hotel organisations possess a huge amount of customer data that can be converted into useful knowledge management. To encapsulate, the hotel industry, like any other industry needs to stay competitive in the dynamic business environment in order to attain success. As a matter of fact, it is crucial for the hotels to understand the patterns of repeat purchase behaviour to retain the customers over a long period of time. The goals and objectives in this direction can only be realized with the use of effective CRM practices for a fruitful relationship between the customers and the organization.

Furthermore, rising customer acquisition costs increased demands of the customers, well-informed consumers, cost-conscious travelers, market uncertainty, and decreased brand loyalty are some of the issues that encourage the hotels to implement CRM as a vital tool.

Customer relationship management is considered to be a strategy that is highly successful in developing and expanding customer base for improving profits through sustained customer loyalty. Researches in the past and present have highlighted the importance of retaining existing customers. Further, organisations have understood that customer retention is by far highly cost-effective than creating new ones. The practice in most of organizations around the world is to build a long-lasting association with the customers for sustainable business. The mantra of success is to focus and channelize all the energy towards economically viable customers.

Hotels need to pay attention to the development of effective CRM as it has the potential to impact customer satisfaction, loyalty and retention by seeking, gathering, storing, validating and communicating relevant data within the organization to optimize profits. In the lieu of the above, it has been rightly said that in order to succeed in the marketplace, hotels need to pay more attention towards addressing the needs and wants of the customers to gain a competitive advantage. In today's time, Customer Relationship Management has largely gained popularity amongst organizations in almost each and every sector. It is in fact one of the vital strategic tools that involve efforts on the part of the managers to manage and build business transactions with clienteles. The main features of CRM implementation can be summarized under three very broad headings: people, systems and processes.

Employee Engagement

Without sufficiently motivated and skilled staff, an organisation cannot create and run customer-focused systems and procedures. Planning for staffing resources must take into account both possible peaks in demand as well as the most anticipated demand. The hallmark of a well-executed CRM deployment is guaranteeing the provision of an exceptional customer experience even in periods of unforeseenly high demand, which calls for the active participation and dedication of all personnel who interact with customers. More and more companies are realising that their workers bring substantial value to the company that goes well beyond just doing their essential tasks.

Employees have a critical role in putting customer service policies into practice, streamlining procedures, and fostering client loyalty. An organization's personnel are rightfully referred to as "our greatest asset" as they are the main source of cost savings, increased productivity, guaranteed quality control, and customer happiness. With businesses putting more of an emphasis on providing exceptional customer experiences, employee engagement is becoming increasingly important

Employee Selection

One has to make sure that the best candidates are chosen in the first place throughout the recruiting process is the first step towards fostering employee engagement. Employers must discover candidates who are ready to learn and stay with the firm in addition to having the requisite abilities because hiring new employees comes with a hefty expense. Giving prospective workers complete and accurate information about the job requirements, expectations, and work environment may significantly increase success rates. If this isn't done, workers may get disillusioned, retention rates may suffer, and word of mouth may become bad as workers advise other prospective hires not to apply for jobs with the firm.

Employers should take extra care when choosing workers who not only have the necessary training and expertise but also have values and goals that align with the company. Technical or task-based aptitudes may often be taught and developed after an individual is hired. The person's psychological traits and work ethic are probably more set in stone. Employers ought to take the stance that "train for skills, recruit for attitude."

Employee Development

Studies have indicated that employees who lack clarity about their job responsibilities experience demotivation, which can result in disgruntled and disloyal customers. As a result, new hires need to be well-prepared for the job that lies ahead of them because their impressions and attitudes towards the organisation are shaped by their early experiences there. It could be necessary for companies without a strong service culture to launch a significant change management initiative that is open to all staff members.

Organisations are adopting more and more internal marketing programs designed to foster customer consciousness and service orientation. The fundamental idea behind internal marketing is to help staff members understand how their actions and attitudes affect clients. This is particularly crucial for staff members who are physically and mentally closest to consumers as well as to one another. Their abilities and focus on the needs of the customer are crucial to the way the client feels about the company and, consequently, influence how loyal they will be in the future.

Employee Empowerment

For employees to provide consumers with higher-quality services, they must be encouraged to use judgement. Change management and employee engagement are closely related since engaging people requires fostering an environment that is conducive to their work. Workers must have the authority to make decisions that affect the direction and performance of the organisation as well as the knowledge necessary to comprehend and contribute to its performance. A quicker and more adaptable response to customers' requirements is given by empowered and engaged staff.

Employee Training & Development

Executive development and staff training are typically included in CRM programs. These activities may fall under the categories of employee engagement or change management, depending on their size and breadth. The first step in every CRM training and development project is a requirements analysis. In order to determine the necessary combination of information, abilities, or attitudes that must be acquired for effective CRM to occur, a comprehensive evaluation will be conducted. It must be carried out by someone with a thorough grasp of the company and the specific training requirements of any CRM system being deployed, and it should be founded on interviews with relevant executives and staff members inside the organisation. Programs for executive development activities usually consist of a number of seminars or gatherings with managers from different departments in the company. This ought to come before staff training and should explain to management the purpose and goals of the organization's CRM programs.

Customer relationship management (CRM) technologies are becoming more and more important in the fast-paced, fiercely competitive hotel sector. Hotels are finding that it is more crucial than ever to invest in CRM software because of the increasing focus on data-driven initiatives and personalised experiences. The capacity of CRM software to customise the customer experience is one of its main advantages. Hotels are able to customise their services to each guest's tastes by gathering and analysing vital consumer data. By providing individualised services and experiences, hotels may go above and beyond the expectations of their guests, from room preferences to special requests.

Hotels can efficiently handle and monitor client data, such as comments and preferences, by utilising CRM systems. Thanks to this abundance of data, hotels are able to offer excellent customer service, respond quickly to issues, and conduct individualised follow-ups. As a result, this degree of client pleasure fosters enduring loyalty and produces favourable word-of-mouth referrals. Hotels may also optimise their marketing strategies with the help of CRM tools. Hotels are better able to create focused marketing campaigns by segmenting their clientele and utilising CRM systems. Hotels can efficiently communicate with potential clients through social media involvement, SMS notifications, and personalised emails.

Effective communication and teamwork are essential in the hotel business, and CRM systems make it easier for hotel employees to communicate with one other. CRM software promotes collaboration across departments and real-time updates for everything from handling requests and room service to sharing vital guest information. Hotels may improve overall operational efficiency through the simplification of operations and the removal of communication gaps. Another benefit of CRM systems is their high rate of client retention. Hotels may use CRM solutions to measure client interaction and establish loyalty programs. Hotels may provide tailored awards, promotions, and incentives to promote customer loyalty and repeat business by keeping an eye on visitor behaviour and preferences. By interacting with previous visitors, targeted email marketing may foster relationships for return visits.

For hotels, Property Management Systems (PMS) and CRM systems must be integrated. Through this connection, processes are streamlined, human data entry is decreased, and correct and up-to-date data is ensured across systems. This results in a single picture of visitor information. Instantaneous access to guest information allows hotel workers to deliver reliable, excellent service. Hoteliers may discover new market niches, decide on pricing, and deploy resources wisely by examining client data, occupancy rates, and revenue patterns. Making decisions based on data is essential to keeping a competitive advantage in the hotel industry.

Hotels must invest in CRM systems due to the fierce

competition in the hospitality sector and the growing significance of data-driven strategies and personalised experiences. Hotels can use the potential of client data, offer tailored experiences, enhance marketing efforts, simplify operations, and increase revenue by utilising CRM software.

Hence, it must be pointed out here that due consideration must be given by the hotel managers in this regard. In their endeavours, the managers may turn their attention towards the internal resources of CRM Organisation, for example, support from the top management, involvement of the employees, organisational structure and application of culture oriented towards the customers to enhance their performance and subsequently to build upon competitive advantage.

Conclusion

A successful CRM implementation requires the involvement and cooperation of your employees. In order to guarantee that your employees feel at ease using the new CRM system, offer assistance and training. Outline the advantages of the CRM system and explain how it will enhance their day-to-day operations. Provide your employees with opportunities to communicate and provide input so they can help the CRM strategy succeed. If required, give them assistance and training to make sure they can use the system well. Demonstrate them how CRM will enhance their day-to-day activities and inspire them to accept the new procedures.

You must examine and improve your company procedures if you want to get the most out of your CRM system. Determine which procedures can be incorporated into the CRM system and made automated. The sales cycle can be streamlined, marketing campaigns can be automated, customer support requests can be handled, and customer interactions can be tracked. The objective is to increase productivity while maintaining the accuracy and consistency of client data. Make sure that client data is of high quality is a crucial component of CRM. Errors and inefficiency can result from poor data quality. To guarantee data accuracy, enforce stringent data entry and validation guidelines. Assign duties for maintaining and updating customer data, and utilise data management technologies to get rid of old and redundant data. It's critical to regularly check for data integrity.

References

- Abdel Fattah Mahmood Al-Azzam. (2016): The Impact of Customer Relationship Management on Hotels Performance in Jordan. International Journal of Business and Social Science, 7(4), 200-210.
- Abdul Alem Mohammad, Basri Bin Rashed & Shaharuddin Bin Tahir (2013): Assessing the influence of Customer Relationship Management (CRM) dimensions on Organisation Performance, An Empirical Study in the Hotel Industry. Journal of Hospitality and Tourism Technology, 4(3), 228-247.
- Abdullateef, A. O., Mokhtar, S. S. & Yusoff, R. Z. (2010): The impact of CRM dimensions on call centre performance. International Journal of Computer Science and Network Security,10, (12), 184-194.
- Abdullateef, A. O., Mokhtar, S. S. M., & Yusoff, R. Z. (2011). The Strategic Impact of Technology-Based CRM on Call Centers' Performance. Journal of Internet Banking and Commerce, 16(1), 1-17
- Acker, Olaf et all. (2011): Social CRM: How Companies Can Link into the Social Web of Consumers. Journal of Direct, Data and Digital Marketing Practice, 13, (1), 3 – 10.
- Ada, S., Lawrence D. Stalcup & Amy Lee (2008): Customer Relationship Management for Hotels in Hong Kong, School of Hotel and Tourism Management, Hong Kong Polytechnic University, Hong Kong, 22(2),139-159.
- Adams, B. (2001): Customer Relationship Management Uncovers Revenues from Loyal Guests. Journal of Hotel and Motel Management, 216 (9), May 21, 36-37.
- Agrawal, M.L. (2001): CRM-From Fad to Strategy, Keynote Address to the CEOs Conclave on CRM, Hyderabad, Nov. 8.
- Agrawal, M.L. (2003): Customer Relationship Management (CRM) and Corporate Renaissance. Journal of Services Research, 3,149–171.
- Akroush, N.M., Dahiyat, E.S., Gharaibeh, S.H., Abu-Lail, N.B. (2011): Customer relationship management implementation. An

investigation of a scale's generalizability and its relationship with business performance in a developing country context. International Journal of Commerce and Management, 21(2), 158-191.
- Alford, P. (2001) eCRM in the travel industry, Travel and Tourism Analyst, Vol.1, No.1, pp.57-76.
- Al Hyari, H.S,., Al Smadi, H.M., & Weshah, S.R. (2023): The Impact of Artificial Intelligence (AI) on Guest Sastifaction in Hotel Management: An Empirical Study of Luxury Hotels. Geo Journal of Tourism and Geosites, 48(2Spl), 810-819.
- Almotairi, M. (2009): A Framework for CRM Success. Proceedings of the European and Mediterranean Conference on Information Systems, Izmir, Turkey, 13-14 July.
- Amoako, G.K., Arthur, E., Bandoh, C. & Katah, R.K. (2012): The Impact of Customer Relationship Management on Repurchase: A Golden Tulip Hotel Study. African Journal of Marketing Management, 4(1), 17-29.
- Anderson, E.W., Forrnell, C., Lehamann, D.R. (1994) Customer Satisfaction, market share and profitability: Findings from Sweden, Journal of Marketing, Vol.58, pp.53-66.
- Ang. L (2011): Community relationship management and social media. Journal of Database Marketing & Customer Strategy Management, (18) 31-38
- Ansuman Sahoo (2020): Emerging Role of Customer Relationship Management in the Hospitality Services: A Study of Hotel Sector in India. International Journal of Management Research and Social Science, 7(4), 126-130.
- Antony, J. & Antony, F.J. (2004): Evaluating Service Quality in a UK Hotel Chain: A Case Study. International Journal of Contemporary Hospitality Management, 16(6), 380-384.
- Aradhana Chadha (2015): Case Study of Hotel Taj in the context of CRM and Customer Retention. Kuwait Chapter. Arabian Journal of Business and Management Review, 4(7), 1-8.
- Armstrong, G. & Kotler, P. (2010) Principles of Marketing 13th, Pearson Education Inc., USA.
- Asikhia, O. (2010): Customer orientation and firm performance among Nigerian small and medium scale businesses. International Journal of Marketing Studies, 2(1), 197-213.
- Atilgan, E., Akinci, S. & Aksoy, S. (2003): Mapping Service Quality in the Tourism Industry. Journal of Managing Service Quality, 13(5), 412-422.
- Babu, Mohan (2003) Business Intelligence - Into the Mind of the

Customer, IT People, Express.
- Banga, G., Kumar, B., & Goyal, H. (2013): Customer relationship management in hotel industry. Pacific Business Review International, 5(12), 71-81.
- Baran, R.J., Galka, R. & Strunk, P.D. (2008): Principles of Customer Relationship Management, Thomson, Mason, OH. Australia South-Western
- Barlett, M.S., (1937): The Statistical Conception of Mental Factors. British Journal of Psychology, 28(1), 97-104.
- Basma Elsaid Eldesouki & Yang Wen (2018): The Impact of CRM Dimensions on the performance of Hotel Industry in Egypt. A Case of Cairo Hotels. International Journal of Business and Management Review, 6(3), 17-44.
- Becker, U.J., Greve, G., Albers, S. (2009): The impact of technological and organizational implementation of CRM on customer acquisition, maintenance, and retention. International Journal of Research in Marketing, 26(3), 207–215.
- Beldi, A., Cheffi, W., Dey, B. (2010): Managing customer relationship management projects: The case of a large French telecommunications company. International Journal of Project Management, 28(4), 339-351.
- Beldona, S., Brewer, P. & Kline, S.F. (2006): Centralized Information Systems in the Lodging Industry: Implications for Knowledge Management. Journal of Information Technology in Hospitality, 4(2), 49-61.
- Beldona, S., Siu, I.S. & Morrison, A. (2006): Trade-off Analysis of Perceived Customer Value: The Case of a Travel Vacation Club. Journal of Hospitality and Leisure Marketing, 14 (3), 65-80.
- Berry, L.L. (1983): Relationship Marketing, Martin Christopher (2002): Relationship marketing Creating Stakeholder Value, Oxford, U.K.; Butterworth Heinemann Ltd.
- Berry, M., & Linoff, S. (2000) Mastering data mining: The art and science of customer relationship management. Wiley Ltd, USA.
- Bettencourt, L.A. (1997) Customer Voluntary Performance: Customers as Partners in Service Delivery. Journal of Retailing, Vol.73, No.3, pp.383-406
- Bharadwaj, A.S. (2000): A Resource-Based Perspective on Information Technology Capability and Firm Performance: An Empirical Investigation. Journal of MIS Quarterly 24(1), 169-196.
- Biggam, S. (2008): Succeeding with your Master's dissertation. England, Open University Press.

- Bland, J. M., & Altman, D. G., (1997): Cronbach's Alpha. British Medical Journal, 314, 572.
- Blattberg, R.C., Kim, B.D, and Neslin, S.A. (2010) Database Marketing: Analyzing and Managing Customers, Springer, USA
- Boon, O., Corbitt, B. and Parker, C. (2002) Conceptualising the requirements of CRM from an organisational perspective: a review of the literature, AWRE 2002: Proceedings of 7th Australian Workshop on Requirements Engineering, pp.83-95
- Bose R. & Sugumaran V. (2003): Application of Knowledge Management Technology in Customer Relationship Management. Journal of Knowledge and Process Management, 10 (1), 3-17.
- Bose R. & Sugumaran V. (2003): Gaining Advantage from Yield Management: Strategic Implementation in the Rapidly Developing World of IT. International Journal of Contemporary Hospitality Management, 17(3), 364- 377.
- Bose, R. (2002): Customer Relationship Management: Key Components for IT Success. Industrial Journal of Management and Data Systems, 102(2), 89-97.
- Boslaugh, Sarah & Paul Andrew Watters (2008): *Statistics in a Nutshell: A Desktop Quick Reference*, ch. 7. Sebastopol, CA: O'Reilly Media.
- Boulding, W., Staelin, R., Ehert, M., and Johnston, W.J. (2005) A CRM Road map: What we know, potential pitfalls, and where to go, Journal of Marketing, Vol.69, No.4, pp.155-166
- Bouncken, R.B. (2002): Knowledge Management for Quality Improvements in Hotels. Journal of Quality Assurance in Hospitality and Tourism, 3(3/4), 25-59.
- Bourne, M. C. S., Neely, A. D., Platts, K. W. & Mills, J. F., (2002): The success and failure of performance measurement initiatives: the perceptions of participating managers. International Journal of Operations and Production Management, 22 (11),1288 – 1310.
- Bowen, J. T., & Shoemaker, S. (1998): Loyalty: A strategic commitment. Cornell Hotel and Restaurant Administration Quarterly, 39(1), 12-25.
- Bradshaw, D. & Brash, C. (2001): Management Customer Relationships in the E Business World, How to Personalize Computer Relationships for Increased Profitability. International Journal of Retail and Distribution Management, 29(12), 520-530.
- Brijesh Kumar Yadav & Abhijeet Singh (2014): Analyzing the Influence of Customer Relationship Management on Firm

Performance: A Study of Hotel Industry in India. International Journal of Customer Relationship Marketing and Management, 5(3), 69-97.
- Brown, T.J., Mowen, J., Todd, D. & Licatta, J. (2002): The customer orientation of service workers: personality trait determinants and effect on self and supervisor performance ratings. Journal of Marketing Research, 39 (1). 110-119.
- Brown. S. (2000): Customer Relationship Management: A Strategic Imperative in the World of e-Business, Wiley
- Brunjes, B. & Roderick, R. (2002): Customer Relationship Management: Why It Does and Does Not Work in South Africa, Paper presented at the IMM Marketing Educators' Conference, South Africa, September.
- Buduiono Hardjono & Lai Povi San (2017): Customer Relationship Management implementation and its Implication to Customer Loyalty in Hospitality Industry. Journal Dinamika Manajemen, 8(1), 92-107.
- Buehrer, R. and Mueller, C.D. (2002) Approach to Overcome Existing Limitations for CRM Implementation, Europe Conference on Information Systems, paper 151, pp.1066-1076.
- Bunthuwun, L., Sirion, C., Howard, C. (2011): Effective Customer relationship management of health care: A study of the perceptions of service quality, cooperate image, satisfaction, and loyalty of that outpatients of private hospital in Thailand. ASBBS Annual Conference: Las Vegas.
- Buttle, F. (2004): Customer Relationship Management: Concepts and Tools Oxford: Elsevier Butterworth-Heinemann.
- Cavalluzzo, K. S., & Ittner, C. D. (2004): Implementing performance measurement innovations: Evidence from government. Accounting, Organizations and Society, 29(3-4),243-267.
- Cavenaghi, V. (2001): Gestão do desempenho empresarial: A contribuição da área de Graduação em Engenharia de Produção, manufatura. Tese (Doutorado em Engenharia de Produção) - Programa de Pós- USP, São Paulo
- Chang, H. & Ku, P. (2009): Implementation of relationship quality for CRM performance: acquisition of BPR and organizational learning, Total Quality Management, 20 (3), 327-348.
- Chang, T.M., Liao, L.L. & Hsiao, W.F. (2005): An empirical study of the e-CRM performance influence model for service sectors in Taiwan, Proceedings of the 2005 IEEE International Conference on e-Technology, e-Commerce and e-Service, pp.

- 240-245, available at: http://ieeexplore.ieee.org/stamp/stamp.jsp?tp¼&arnumber¼1402302& userType¼instv (accessed May 28, 2011).
- Chang, W., Park, J.E., & Chairy, S (2010): How does CRM Technology transform into organisational performance? A Mediating Role of Marketing Capability. Journal of Business Research, 63(8), 849-855.
- Chaudhuri, A. & Shainesh, I. (2001): Implementing a Technology Based CRM Solution. Tata: McGraw-Hill.
- Chen, I.J. & Popovich, K. (2003): Understanding Customer Relationship Management (CRM): People, Process and Technology, Business Process Management Journal, 9(5), 672-688.
- Chen, I.J. and Popovich, K. (1997) Understanding customer relationship management (CRM): People, process and technology, Business Process Management Journal, Vol.5, No.5, pp.672-688.
- Chi, C.G. Q. & Qu, H. (2008): Examining the Structural Relationships of Destination Image, Tourist Satisfaction and Destination Loyalty: An Integrated Approach. Journal of Tourism Management, 29,624-636.
- Cho, H., & Pucik, V. (2005): Relationship between innovativeness, quality, growth, profitability, and market value. Strategic Management Journal, 26(6), 555-575.
- Choi T. Y., & Chu R. (2001): Determinants of hotel guests' satisfaction and repeat patronage in Hong Kong hotel industry. International Journal of Hospitality Management, 20(3), 277-297.
- Chon, K.S. & Sparrowe, R.T. (2000): Welcome to Hospitalty: An Introduction, *Delmar* Cengage Learning; 2nd edition
- Chou, C.D., Lin, B., Xu,Y. & Yen C.D. (2002): Adopting Customer Relationship Management Technology. Journal of Industrial Management and Data Systems, 102(8), 442-452.
- Christou, E. (2000): Guest Loyalty Likelihood in Relation to Hotels' Corporate Image and Reputation: A Study of Three Countries in Europe. Journal of Hospitality and Leisure Marketing, 10(1), 88-99.
- Christou, E., & Kassianidis, P. (2003): Consumer Perception and Adoption of online Buying For Travel Products. Journal of Travel and Tourism Marketing, 12(4), 93-107
- Cline, R. & Rach, L. (2000): Hospitality 2000: A View to the Next Millennium, Arthur Anderson and New York University, New York.
- Collins, C. & Buhalis, D. (2003): Destination Management Systems Utilization in England, in Information and Communication Technologies in Tourism: Proceedings of the International Conference in Helsinki, Finland: 202-211.

- Comfort M.Klutse (2016): Relationship Management in Hospitality Industry: The Case of hotels in Ghana. Global Journal of Commerce & Management Perspective, 5(1), 12-15.
- Cross, R. & Janet, S. (1996): Customer Bonding Pathway to Lasting Customer Loyalty, Contemporary Publishing, Chicago, USA.
- Croteau, A.M. & Li, P. (2003): Critical success factors of CRM technological initiatives. Canadian Journal of Administrative Sciences, 20 (1), 21-34.
- Currie, Marla (2013): (e How Contributor), Theories on the promotional Mix, www.eHow.com/info_8340520_theories_promotional_mix.html
- Daft, R.L. (2006): The new era of management, Ohio: International Edition. Mason: South-Western Thomson
- Davenport, T. H., & Beers, M. C. (1995): Managing information about processes. Journal of Management Information Systems, 12(1),57– 80.
- Day, G. S., & Van den Bulte, C. (2002): Superiority in customer relationship management: Consequences for competitive advantage and performance, Working paper, Wharton School of Economics, University of Pennsylvania.
- Demand Media (2013): What Is Customer Relations by Contributing Writer, http://smallbusiness.chron.com/customer-relations-43230.html
- Dev, C. & Olsen, M.D. (2000): Marketing Challenges for the Next Decade, Journal of Cornell Hotel and Restaurant Administration Quarterly, 42(1),41–47.
- Dewnarain, S., Ramkissoon, H., & Mavondo, F. (2018): Social customer relationship management: An integrated conceptual framework. Journal of Hospitality Marketing & Management, 28(2), 172–188
- Dickinson, C. (2006): Transformation in the Lodging Industry, Journal of Lodging Hospitality, 62(8), 60-63.
- Dickinson, C.B. (2001): CRM-Enhanced Revenue Management in the Hospitality Industry, Hospitality Upgrade, summer, 136,138.
- Diffley, S., McCole, P., & Carvajal-Trujillo, E. (2018): Examining social customer relationship management among Irish hotels. International Journal of Contemporary Hospitality Management, 30(2), 1072–1091.
- Dimitriadis, S. & Steven, E. (2008): Integrated customer relationship management for service activities: an internal/external gap model, Managing Service Quality, 18 (5), 496-511.

- Dinesh Kumar & Pawan Kumar (2017): CRM: Impact on Hotel Industry. International Journal of Advanced Research and Development, 2(5), 929-932.
- Dominici, G. & Guzzo, R. (2010): Customer Satisfaction in the hotel industry: A case study from Sicily, International Journal of Marketing Studies, 2(2), 3-12.
- Dowling, J. (1993): Organizational legitimacy: social values and organizational behavior. Pacific Sociological Review, 18,(122-136).
- Drucker, P. (1999): Management Challenges for the 21st Century, Harper Business, New York.
- Duggan, T. (2013): The Top Customer Service Management Skills for Hiring Managers, Demand Media, http://work.chron.com/
- Dutu, C. & Halmajan, H. (2011): The effect of organizational readiness on CRM and business performance. International Journal of Computers, 1 (2), 106-114.
- Dwyer, R., Schurr, P. & Oh, S. (1987): Developing Buyer-Seller Relations, Journal of Marketing, 51(2),11-27.
- Dyché, J. (2000): e- Data: Turning Data Into Information With Data Warehousing, Addison-Wesley.
- Dyché, J. (2002): The CRM Handbook: A business Guide to Customer relationship management, Boston: Addison-Wesley.
- Eid, R. (2007): Towards a Successful CRM Implementation in Banks: An Integrated Model. The Service Industries Journal, 27(8), 1021–1039. European Journal of Marketing, 39(11/12), 1264-1290.
- Ekinci, Y. (2002): A Review of Theoretical Debates on the Measurement of Service Quality: Implications for Hospitality Research, Journal of Hospitality & Tourism Research, 26(3): 199-216.
- Elahi Taghavi Shavazi, Asghar Moshabaki, Seyyed Hamid Khodabad Hoseini & Asadolla Kord Naiej (2013): Customer Relationship Management And Organizational Performance: A Conceptual Framework Based On The Balanced Scorecard (Study Of Iranian Banks). IOSR Journal of Business & Management, 10(6), 18-26.
- Elmuti, D., Jia, H. & Gray, D. (2009): Customer relationship management strategic application and organizational effectiveness: an empirical investigation. Journal of Strategic Marketing, 17(1), 75-96.
- Engstrom, T.E., Westnes, P. & Westnes, S.F. (2003): Evaluating Intellectual Capital in the Hotel Industry. Journal of Intellectual Capital, 4(3), 287-303.
- Ernst, H., Hoyer, D.W., Krafft, M. & Krieger, K. (2011): Customer relationship management and company performance – the

- mediating role of new product performance. Journal of the Academy of Marketing Science, 39(2), 290-306.
- Fan, F. (2011): The Impact of Customer Service through information systems for the Lodging Industry. Available: www.jgbm.org/page/6%20Edward%20C.S.%20Ku%20.pdf. (Accessed 27 April, 2020).
- Fan, Y. & Ku, E. (2010): Customer focus, service process fit and customer relationship management profitability: the effect of knowledge sharing. The Service Industries Journal, 30 (2), 203-222.
- Field, A. (2005): Discovering Statistics Using SPSS, 2nd ed., Sage, London.
- Fjermestad,J. and Romand, N.C. (2006) Electronic customer relationship management, JR, M.E.Sharpe. Inc, USA.
- Fornell, C. (1992) A national customer satisfaction barometer: The Swedish experience, Journal of Marketing, Vol.56, pp.6-21.
- Fox, T. & Stead, S. (2001): Customer relationship management: delivering the benefits, White Paper, CRM (UK) and SECOR Consulting, New Malden, available at: www.iseing. org/emcis/EMCISWebsite/EMCIS2011%20Proceedings/SCI10.pdf (accessed July 24, 2020).
- Franco-Santos, M. & Bourne, M., Kennerley, M. (2005): Managing through measures: a study of impact on performance. Journal of Manufacturing Technology Management, 16(4),373-395
- Fu, Y.Y. & Parks, S.C. (2001): The Relationship Between Restaurant Service Quality and Customer Loyalty among the Elderly, Journal of Hospitality and Tourism Research, 25(3), 320-336.
- Fukey Leena, Jaykumar & Surya Sarah Issac (2015): Assessing CRM Practices in Hotel Industry: A Look at the Progress and Prospects. Indian Journal of Science and Technology, 8(S6), 82-90.
- Gamble, P., Chalder, M. & Stone, M. (2001): Customer Relationship Management in the Travel Industry, Journal of Vacation Marketing, 7(1), 83-91.
- Gilbert, D. C., Powell-Perry, J., & Widijoso, S. (1999): Approaches by hotels to the use of the Internet as a relationship marketing tool. Journal of Marketing Practice: Applied Marketing Science, 5(1), 21-38.
- Gil-Gomez, H. , Guerola-Navarro, V. , Oltra-Badenes, R. ,& Lozano-Quilis, J. A. (2020): Customer Relationship Management: Digital transformation and suitable business model innovation. Economic Research-Ekonomska Istraživanja, 33 (1), 2733–2750

- Gil-Gomez, H. Guerola-Navarro, V. , & Oltra-Badenes, R. Y. (2020b): Análisis de la relación entre el grado de introducción de CRM y los beneficios de la empresa a través del Desempeño Organizacional y la Innovación Empresarial. 3C Empresa. Investigación y Pensamiento Crítico , 9 (1), 67–65.
- Gilmore, A. (2003): Services Marketing and Management, SAGE publications Ltd, UK.
- Go, F. M. & Govers, R. (2000): Integrated Quality Management for Tourist Destinations: A European Perspective on Achieving Competitiveness, Journal of Tourism Management, 21(1): 79-88.
- Goodhue, D. L. (1995): Understanding user evaluations of information systems, Journal of Management Science, 41(12), 1827-1844.
- Goulian, C. & Mersereau, A. (2000): Performance measurement- implementing a corporate scorecard, Ivey Business Journal, 65 (1), 48-54.
- Gray, P. and Byun, J. (2001) Customer Relationship Management, Center for research on information technology and organizations, Version 3-6, available at: http://www.crito.uci.edu/papers/2001/crm.pdf.
- Green, P.R., & Stager, J.C. (2005): Techniques and methods of GIS for business, in Pick.
- Greenberg, P. (2001): CRM at the Speed of Light: Capturing and Keeping Customers in Internet Real Time, Osborne/McGraw-Hill, Berkeley, California.
- Greenberg, P., (2004): CRM at the Speed of Light: Capturing and Keeping Customers in Internet Real Time, McGraw-Hill, Berkeley, CA.
- Gronroos, C. (2004): The relationship marketing process: communication, interaction, dialogue, value. Journal of Business and Industrial Marketing,19(2),99-113.
- Gruen T. W., Summers J. O., & Acito, F. (2000): Relationship marketing activities, commitment, and membership behaviors in professional associations. Journal of Marketing, 64 (3): 34-49.
- Gujrati, Rashmi (2016): 'CRM for Reatailers: Business Intelligence in Retail CRM', International Journal of Applied Research, 2, (1), 24-29.
- Gummesson, E., (1997): Relationship Marketing as a paradigm shifts: Some conclusion from the 30R. Approach, Journal of Management Decision, 35(4), 267-272
- Gupta, S., Lehmann, D.R. & Stuart, J.A. (2001): Valuing Customers,

- Journal of Marketing Science Institute Report No. 01-119.
- Hair, J.F., Black, W.C., Babin, B.J., Anderson, R.E. & Tatham, R.L. (2010): Multivariate Data Analysis a Global Perspective, 7th ed., Pearson Education, Upper Saddle River, NJ.
- Haley, M. & Watson, B. (2002): The ABCs of CRM: Part One of Two, Hospitality Upgrade, summer, 36(4): 40-52.
- Hallin, C.A. & Marnburg, E. (2008): Knowledge management in the hospitality industry: a review of empirical research, Tourism Management, 29 (2), 366-381.
- Hallowell, R. (1996) The relationship of customer satisfaction, customer loyalty and profitability: an empirical study, International Journal of Service Industry Management, Vol.7, No.4, pp.27-42.
- Hamann.H., Schiemann.F., Lucia. B.B., & Thomas. W.G. (2013): Exploring the Dimensions of Organisational Performance: A Construct Validity Study. Organisational Research Methods, 16(1), 67-87.
- Hamid, H. (2009): "Toward unfolding CRM implementation in Pakistan: a case study", paper presented at 17th European Conference on Information Systems, Islamabad, available at: http://is2.lse.ac.uk/asp/aspecis/20090249.pdf (accessed June 28, 2011).
- Hamid, N.R., Cheng, A.W. & Akhir, R.M. (2011): A Global competitive advantage, Journal of Innovation and Knowledge Management, 21, (2), 72-84.
- Hammer, M. (1996): Beyond Reengineering: How the Process-Centered Organization Is Changing Our Work And Our Lives, New York: HarperCollins.
- Haraketi, T. (2011): Effective Hotel Distribution Channels Management, June 4th, http://www.blogcatalog.com/post/0e2b705752a113b12e15cb839b8940eb
- Hardik Panchal & Rushab Shah (2018): The impact of Effective Customer Relationship Management in Hotel Industry. Internal Journal of Advance Research and Innovative Ideas in Education, 4(6), 262-265.
- Hermans, O. (2009): Customer Relationship Management & Performance Management: Exploring an Actionable Link in Hospitality, Journal of Hospitality Research, 4(1), 19-27.
- Heung, V.C.S., Wong, M.Y. & Qu, H. (2000): Airport-Restaurant Service Quality in Hong Kong: An Application of Servqual, The Cornell Hotel and Restaurant Administration Quarterly, 41(3), 86-96.
- Hippner, H. (2006): Grundlagen des CRM Konzepte und Gestaltung,

- Gabler Publisher, Wiesbaden, (2nd Ed.), in Fuzzy classification of online customers, by Nicolas Werro (2008): Ph.D. Thesis, submitted to the university of Fribourg (Switzerland).
- Hofstede, G. (2001): Culture's Consequences: Comparing Values, Behavior, Institutions and Organizations across Nations. Thousand Oaks, CA: Sage (co published in the PRC as Vol. 10.
- Holjevac, Ivanka Avelini, Suzana Marković & Sanja Raspor (2007): Customer Satisfaction Measurement In Hotel Industry: Content Analysis Study.
- Holme, I.M. & Solvand, B.K. (1991): Forskningsmetodik: Om Kvalitativa och Kvantitativa Metoder. Lund, Sverige: Studentlitteratur.
- Hossein, N.M., & Zakaria, N.H., (2012): CRM Benefits for Customers: Literature Reivew (2005-2012). International Journal of Engineering Research and Applications, 2(6), 1578-1586.
- Hui, K.C. (2006). Relationship Marketing: Is It a Paradigm Shift? Available at: http://kchui.com/articles/Relationship_Marketing_Paradigm_Shift.pdf.
- Hung, Y.S., Hung, H.W., Tsai, A.C., Jiang, C.S. (2010): Critical factors of hospital adoption on CRM system: organizational and information system perspective. Decision support systems,48.
- Hussain, I., Hussain, M., Hussain, S., Sajid, M. (2009): Customer Relationship Management: Strategies and Practices in Selected Banks of Pakistan. International Review of Business in hotel industry. International Journal of Economics and Management, 3(2), 297 – 316.
- Hussein M. Hussein Ibrahim (2021). The Analysis of Implementation of Customer Relationship Management on Five Star Hotels in North Cyprus. Annals of R.S.C.B, 25(6), 3676-3693.
- Hyun, S. S., & Perdue, R. R. (2017): Understanding the dimensions of customer relationships in the hotel and restaurant industries. International Journal of Hospitality Management, 64, 73–84.
- Imrie, R. & Fyall, A. (2000): Customer Retention and Loyalty in the Independent Mid-Market Hotel Sector: A United Kingdom Perspective, Journal of Hospitality and Leisure Marketing, 7 (3): 39-54.
- Inge, J. (2001): Customer Relationship Management: Is Your Approach Successful? Hospitality Upgrade, Fall, 8, 10, 12, 14, 16, 18.
- Jani, D. & Han, H. (2013): Personality, social comparison, consumption emotions, satisfaction, and behavioral intentions: How do these and other factors relate in a hotel setting?" International

Journal of Contemporary Hospitality Management, 25 (7), 970- 993.
- Jayachandran, S., Sharma, S., Kaufman, P. & Raman, P. (2005): The Role of Relational Information Processes and Technology Use in Customer Relationship Management, Journal of Marketing, 69(4):177-192.
- Jones D. L., Mak B., & Sim J. (2007): A New Look at the Antecedents and Consequences of Relationship Quality in the Hotel Service Environment. Services Marketing Quarterly, 28(3): 15-31.
- Jones, D. L. & McCleary, K.W. (2005): An Empirical Approach to Identifying Cross-Cultural Modifications to International Hospitality Industry Sales Training, Journal of Travel and Tourism Marketing, 18(4), 65-81.
- Jones, P. (2002): Introduction to Hospitality Operations, London, Continuum.
- Julnes, P. d. L., & Holzer, M. (2001): Promoting the utilization of performance measures in public organizations: An empirical study of factors affecting adoption and implementation. PublicAdministration Review, 61(6), 693-708.
- Jung, S. (2003): The effects of organizational culture on conflict resolution in marketing, Journal of American Academy of Business, 11(3), 242-246.
- Juwaheer, T.D. (2004): Exploring International Tourists' Perceptions of Hotel Operations by Using a Modified Servqual Approach - A Case Study of Mauritius, Journal of Managing Service Quality,14(5),350-364.
- Kaiser (1974): An index of factorial simplicity. Psychometrical, 39(31-36).
- Kamath, K. V., Kohli, S. S., Shenoy, P. S., Kumar, R., Nayak, R. M., Kuppuswamy, P. T., & Ravichandran, N. (2003). Indian banking sector: Challenges and opportunities. Vikalpa, 28(3), 83-100
- Kamath, V., Bhonsale, S. & Manjrekar, P. (2008): Customer Relationship Management: A Case Study of Tourism Services in Navi Mumbai, Paper presented in the conference on Tourism in India – Challenges Ahead, 15-17, May 2008, IIMK, Mumbai.
- Kandampully, J. & Suhartanto, D. (2000): Customer Loyalty in The Hotel Industry: The Role of Customer Satisfaction and Image, International Journal of Contemporary Hospitality Management, 12(6), 346-351.
- Kaplan, R. S., & Norton, D. P. (2001): The Strategy focused organization: How balanced scorecard companies thrive in the new business environment. Boston, Harvard Business School Press.

- Kaplan, R. S., & Norton, D.P. (1992): The balanced scorecard – measures that drive performance. Harvard Business Review 70 (1), 71-79.
- Kaplan, R.S. & Norton, D.P. (1996): Using the balanced scorecard as a strategic management system, Harvard Business Review, 74 (1), 75-85.
- Kaplan, R.S. & Norton, D.P. (2001): Transforming the balanced scorecard from performance measurement to strategic management: part I, Accounting Horizons, 15 (1), 87-104.
- Kaplan, R.S. & Norton, D.P. (2004): Measuring the strategic readiness of intangible assets, Harvard Business Review, 82 (2), 52-63.
- Karimi, J., Somers, T. & Gupta, Y. (2001): Impact of Information Technology Management Practices on Customer Service, Journal of Management Information Systems, 17(4), 125-158.
- Kasim, Nor Aziah Abu & Badriyah Minai (2009): Linking CRM Strategy, Customer Performance Measures and Performance in the Hotel Industry, Int. Journal of Economics and Management, 3(2), 297 – 316.
- Katarzyna Tworek & Anna Salamacha (2019): CRM Influence on Organisational Performance – The Moderating Role of IT Reliability. Engineering Management in Production and Services, 11(3), 96-105.
- Kaur P, Stoltzfus J, Yellapu V (2018): Descriptive Statistics. Int J Acad Med, 4(1), 60-63.
- Kelly. K., Clark. B., Brown.V., & Sitzia.J. (2003): Good Practice in the conduct and reporting of Survey Research. International Quality Health Care, 15(3), 261-266.
- Kennedy, K.N., Lassk, F.G. & Goolsby, J.R. (2002): Customer mind-set of employees throughout the organization, Journal of the Academy of Marketing Science, 30 (2), 159-171.
- Kharbanda V & Dasgupta P (2001): Data Mining for Customer Relationship Management. Decision 28,127-138.
- Kim W. G., Han J. S., & Lee E. (2001): Effects of relationship marketing on repeat purchase and word of mouth. Journal of Hospitality & Tourism Research, 25 (3), 272-288.
- Kim, B.Y. (2008): Mediated effects of customer orientation on customer relationship management performance, International Journal of Hospitality & Tourism Administration, 9 (2), 192-218.
- Kim, J., Suh, E. & Hwang, H. (2003): A Model for Evaluating The Effectiveness of CRM Using the Balanced Scorecard, Journal of Interactive Marketing, 17(2), 5–19.
- Kim, W., Ok, C., & Gwinner, K. P. (2010): The antecedent role

- of customer-to-employee relationships in the development of customer-to-firm relationships. The Service Industries Journal, 30(7), 1139–1157.
- Kimes, S.E. (2002): Perceived fairness of yield management-part two, The Cornell Hotel and Restaurant Administration Quarterly, 43(1), 22-29.
- Kohli, R., Piontek, F., Ellington, T., VanOsdol, T., Shepard, M., & Brazel, G. (2001): ―Managing customer relationships through ebusiness decision support applications: A case of hospital–physician collaboration‖, Decision Support Systems, 32, (2), 171–187.
- Kotler P. (1997): Marketing Management: Analysis, Planning, Implementation and Control, Prentice- Hall, Englewood Cliffs, NJ.
- Kotler, P. (2000): Marketing Management, The Millennium Edition, (10th Ed.), Prentice Hall.
- Kotler, P. (2002): When to Use CRM and When to Forget it! Paper Presented at the Academy of Marketing Science, Sanibel Harbour Resort and Spa, 30 May.
- Kotler, P. and Keller, K.L. (2011) Marketing Management 14th edition, Pearson Education, UK.
- Kotler, P., Bowen, J. & Makens, J. (2003): Marketing for Hospitality and Tourism (3rd Ed.), Upper Saddle River, NJ: Prentice Hall.
- Kotorov, R. (2003): Customer Relationship Management: Strategic Lessons and Future Directions, Business Process Management Journal, 9(5), 566-571.
- Kracklauer, A.H. & Mills, D.Q. (2004): Collaborative Customer Relationship Management: Taking CRM to the Next Level, Springer, Berlin.
- Krasnikov, A., Jayachandran, S., Kumar,V. (2009): The Impact of Customer Relationship Management Implementation on Cost and Profit Efficiencies: Evidence from the U.S. Commercial Banking Industry. Journal of Marketing, 73(6), 61-77.
- Kriegl, U. (2000): International Hospitality Management, Cornell Hotel and Restaurant Administration Quarterly, 41(2): 64-71.
- Krishnan, Vijaykumar et al. 2014: Linking Customer Relationship Management (CRM) Processes to Sales Performance: The Role of CRM Technology Effectiveness, The Marketing Management Journal, 24(2), 162 – 171.
- Ku, E.C.S. (2010): The impact of customer relationship management through implementation of information systems, Total Quality Management & Business Excellence, 21 (11), 1085-1102.

- Kueng, P. (2002): Performance measurement systems in the service sector: the potential of IT is not yet utilised. International Journal of Business Performance Management, 4(1), 95-114.
- Kumar Yadav, B. (2013): Customer Relationship Management Implementation Strategies in Hotel Industry, MERC Global's International Journal of Management, 1 (2), 103-119.
- Kumar, A. (2012) Cross selling with Special Reference to State Bank of India, International Journal of social sciences &interdisciplinary research, Vol. 1, No. 6, pp. 116-123
- Kumar, B., Banga, G., & Thapar, J. (2012): An Assessment of Service Quality of Hotel Industry, A Refereed Quarterly Journal, 4(1), 13-30
- Kumar, V. & Reinartz, W.J. (2006): Customer Relationship Management: A Database Approach, Hoboken, NJ: John Wiley and Sons.
- Kumar, V., Lemon, K. N. & Parasuraman, A. (2006): Managing Customers for Value: An Overview and Research Agenda, Journal of Service Research, 9(2), 87–94.
- Lam T., & Zhang H. (1999): Service quality of travel agents: the case of travel agents in Hong Kong. Tourism Management, 20(3),341–349.
- Lawson-Body, A., & Limayem, M. (2004): The impact of customer relationship management on customer loyalty: The moderating role of web site characteristics. Journal of Computer-Mediated Communication, 9(4).
- Lee, S., Su, H. & Dubinsky, A.J. (2005): Relationship Selling in the Meeting Planner/ Hotel Salesperson Dyad. Journal of Hospitality & Tourism Research, 29(4)
- Lee, Y. K., Jeong, Y. K., & Choi, J. (2014): Service quality, relationship outcomes, and membership types in the hotel industry: A survey in Korea. Asia Pacific Journal of Tourism Research, 19(3), 300–324.
- Lefebure R. & Venturi G. (2000): Gestion de la Relation Client, Editions Eyrolles, Paris, Hotel Salesperson Dyad. Journal of Hospitality and Tourism Research, 29(4), 427-447.
- Li, R.M (2009) How to use the CRM system implement cross-selling, Fazhiyujingji Journal, Vol.215, No.9, pp.100-101.
- Lin, Y., & Su, H. (2003): Strategic analysis of Customer Relationship Management - a field study on hotel enterprises. Total Quality Management, 14(6), 715-731.
- Lindgreen, A., and Crawford, I., (1999) Implementing, monitoring and measuring a programme of relationship marketing Marketing Intelligence and Planning, Marketing Intelligence & Planning,

- Vol.17, No.5, pp. 231–239.
- Ling, R. & Yen, D.C. (2001) Customer Relationship Management: An Analysis Framework and Implementation Strategies. The Journal of Computer Information Systems, 41(3): 82-97.
- Lipton, M. (2003): Guiding growth: How vision keeps companies on Course. Boston, Harvard Business School Press.
- Liu, H.-Y. (2007): Development of a framework for customer relationship management (CRM) in the banking industry. International Journal of Management, 24 (1)15-32.
- Liu, S.S., Luo, X. & Shi, Y. (2003): Market oriented organizations in an emerging economy: a study of the missing links. Journal of Business Research, 56 (6), 481-491.
- Liz Lee Kelly, David Gilbert & Robin Mannicom (2003): How e-CRM can enhance Customer Loyalty. Marketing Intelligence & Planning, 21(4), 239-248.
- Lo, A.S., Stalcup, L.D. & Lee, A. (2010): Customer relationship management for hotels in Hong Kong. International Journal of Contemporary Hospitality Management, 22 (2), 139-159.
- Lo, Ada. S. Lawrence D. Stalcup & Amy Lee (2008): Customer Relationship Management for Hotels in Hong Kong, Emerald Group Publishing Limited, Hong Kong.
- Luck, D., & Lancaster, G. (2013): The significance of CRM to the strategies of hotel companies. Worldwide Hospitality and Tourism Themes, 5(1), 55-66.
- Luck, D., & Stephenson, M.L. (2009): An Evaluation of the Significant Elements of Customer Management within the Hotel Industry. Tourism Today, 9, 7-26.
- Lund, D.B. (2003): Organizational culture and job satisfaction. Journal of Business and Industrial Marketing, 18(3), 219-236.
- Magnini, V. P., Honeycutt, E. D., Jr. & Hodge, S. K. (2003): Data Mining for Hotel Firms: Use and Limitations. Cornell Hotel and Restaurant Administration Quarterly, 44 (2), 94-105.
- Mahesh Chhaburao Wilayate & Deshmukh R.P. (2014): To Study Customer Relationship Management in Hospitality Industry. IBMRD's Journal of Management and Research, 3(1), 151-163.
- Mantu Kakati (2019): Tourism Industry – A Fastest Growing Tertiary Sector in Assam: An Explorative Research. Addiyan Journal of Arts Humanities & Social Sciences, 2(1).
- Marković, S. (2004): Measuring Service Quality in Croatian Hotel Industry: A Multivariate Statistical Analysis. Our Economy, 1/2:27-35.

- Marković, S. (2005): Perceived Service Quality Measurement in Tourism Higher Education: Case study of Croatia. Tourism Today, Fall: 91-109.
- Martis, Clifford (2000): Consumerism-Key to the New Millennium, In (Ed), K. Anantharama Rao, Vision 21st Century. Vidya Publishing House, Mangalore, India, 450-455.
- Mazumdar, T. (1993) A Value-based orientation to new production planning, Journal of Customer Marketing, Vol.10, Iss.1, pp.28-41
- McKenna, R. (1991) Relationship Marketing, Perseus Book, USA
- Mechinda, P. & Patterson, P.G. (2011): The impact of service climate and service provider personality on employees' customer-oriented behavior in a high-contact setting. Journal of Services Marketing, 25 (2), 101-113.
- Mehta D., Sharma J. K., & Mehta N. (2010): A Study of Customer Relationship 65 Management Practices in Madhya Pradesh State Tourism Services, Theoretical and Applied Economics Volume 16, 5(546), 73-80.
- Mguyen, T.U.H., Sherif, J. S., & Newby, M. (2007): Strategies for successful CRM implementation. Information Management and Computer Security, 15(2), 102-15.
- Miller, B. A., & Swope, S. (2007): Assessing Organizational Performance in Higher Education. International Journal of Educational Advancement. 16(3), 258-263.
- Minghetti, V. (2003): Building customer value in the hospitality industry: towards the definition of a customer-centric. Journal of Information Technology & Tourism, 6 (2), 141-152.
- Mishra, A., & Rath. S. (2024). CRM in Tourism Sector: A Case Analysis. International Journal of Research Publication and Reviews, 5(5), 2384-2387.
- Mittal, V. & Kamakura, W.A. (2001): Satisfaction, Repurchase Intent and Repurchase Behavior: Investigating the Moderating Effect of Customer Characteristics, Journal of Marketing Research, 39:131-142.
- Mohammed T. Nuseir & Ghaleb El Refae (2022): The Effect of Digital Marketing Capabilities on Business Performance Enhancement: Mediating the Role of Customer Relationship Management. International Journal of Data and Network Science, 6(2), 295-304
- Mohammed, A.A. & Rashid, B (2012): Customer Relationship Management in Hotel industry: A framework Proposal on the Relationship among CRM Dimensions, Marketing Capabilities and Hotel Performance. International Review of Management and

- Marketing, 2(4), 220-230.
- Mohammed, N. U. (2012): Customer relationship management in hospitality sector. Journal of Good Governance and Sustainable Development, 1(1),40-47.
- Mohammed, N.U. (2012) Customer relationship management in hospitality sector. Journal of good governance and sustainable development, Vol.1, No.1, pp.40-47.
- Moreno, G.A. & Melendez, P.A. (2011): Analyzing the impact of knowledge management on CRM success: the mediating effects of organizational factors. International Journal of Information Management, 31, 437-444.
- Morgan, R. M., & Hunt, S.D. (1994): The commitment-trust theory of relationship marketing. Journal of Marketing, 58(3), 20-38.
- Moriarty, J., Jones, R., Rowley, J. & Kupiec-Teahan, B. (2008): Marketing in small hotels: a qualitative study. Marketing Intelligence & Planning, 26 (3), 293-315.
- Muhammed Nuseira and Ghaleb El Refaea (2022), The effect of digital marketing capabilities on business performance enhancement: Mediating the role of customer relationship management (CRM). International Journal of Data and Network Science, 6, 295–304
- Mukerjee, K. & Singh, K. (2009): CRM: a strategic approach. Journal of Management Research, 8 (2), 65-82.
- Mumel, D. & Snoj, B. (2007): The Analysis of Questionnaires for Hotel Guests Satisfaction - Comparison Between Croatia and Slovenia, 4th International Conference Global Challenges for Competitiveness: Business and Government Perspective, Juraj Dobrila University of Pula, Pula, Croatia: 564- 575.
- Mwangi Charles Gacheru, Rayviscici Ndivo Mutinda & Evangeline Gichunge (2019): Influence of Customer Relationship Management Dimensions on Performance of Classified Accommodation Facilities in Kenya. IOSR Journal of Business and Management, 21(6), 11-16.
- Mylonakis, J. (2009): Customer relationship management functions: A survey of Greek bank customer satisfaction perceptions. The Icfai University Journal of Bank Management, 8(2), 7-31.
- Nagwan AlQershi, Sany Sanuri Mohd Mokhtar & Zakaria Bin Abas (2020): Innovative CRM and Performance of SMEs: The Moderating Role of Relational Capital. Journal of Open Innovation: Technology, Marketing and Complexity, 6(155), 1-18.
- Namkung, Y. & Jang, S. (2008): Are Highly Satisfied Restaurant Customers Really Different? A Quality Perception Perspective. International Journal of Contemporary Hospitality Management,

20(2), 142-155.
- Narver, J.C. & Slater, S.F. (1990): The effect of a market orientation on business profitability, Journal of Marketing, 45(4), 20-36.
- Nasution, H.N., Mavondo, F.T. (2008): Organizational capabilities: antecedents and implications for customer value. European Journal of Marketing, 42(3/4), 477-501.
- Nemati, H.R., Barko, C.D. & Moosa, A. (2003): e-CRM Analytics: The Role of Data Integration, International Journal of Electronic Commerce in Organizations, 1(13), 73–89.
- Ngai, E.W.T. (2005): Customer relationship management research (1992-2002): an academic literature review and classification. Marketing Intelligence Planning, 23(6), 582-605.
- Nickson, D. (2007): Human Resource Management for the Hospitality and Tourism Industries, Elsevier.
- Noone, Breffni M., Sheryl E., Kimes & Leo M. Renaghan (2003): Integrating Customer Relationship Management and Revenue Management: A Hotel Perspective. Journal of Revenue and Pricing Management, 2, (7-21)
- Nudurupati, S. S., & Bititci, U. S. (2005): Implementation and impact of IT-supported performance measurement systems. Production Planning & Control, 16(2):152-162.
- Nunnally, J.C. (1978) Psychometric theory. 2nd Edition, McGraw-Hill, New York.
- Olsen, M.D. (1996): Events shaping the future and their impact on the multinational hotel Industry. Tourism Recreation Research, 21(2): 7-14.
- O'Neill, J.W. & Mattila, A.S. (2010): Hotel brand strategy, Cornell Hospitality Quarterly, 51, (1), 27-34.
- Osama Omar Abobark & Ramanthan Kalimuthu.K (2019): A Review of Factors of Customer Relationship Management and their Impact on Hotel Performance. International Advanced Research Jouirnal in Science, Engineering and Technology, 6(2), 64-66.
- Osarenkhoe, A. & Bennai, E.A. (2007), An exploratory study of implementation of customer relationship management strategy. Business Process Management Journal, 13 (1), 139-164.
- Özgener, Ş., & İraz, R. (2006): Customer relationship management in small–medium enterprises: The case of Turkish tourism industry. Tourism Management, 27(6), 1356-1363.
- Padmanabhan, B. & Tuzhilin, A. (2003) On the Use of Optimization for Data Mining: Theoretical Interactions and e-CRM Opportunities, Journal of Management Science, 49:1327-1343.

- Pallant, J. (2007): SPSS Survival Manual: A Step by Step Guide to Data Analysis Using SPSS for Windows (Version 15), 3rd ed., Open University Wadsworth, New York, NY.
- Palmer, A., McMahon-Beattie, U. & Beggs, R. (2000): A Structural Analysis of Hotel Sector Loyalty Programs. International Journal of Contemporary Hospitality Management, 12(1), 54-60.
- Papastathopoulou, P., Avlonitis, G., Panagopoulos N.G. (2007): Intra organizational information and communication technology diffusion: implications for industrial sellers and buyers. Industrial Marketing Management, 36(3), 322-336.
- Paraskevas, A. & Buhalis, D. (2002): Outsourcing IT for Small Hotels: The Opportunities and Challenges of Using Application Service Providers. The Cornell Hotel and Restaurant Administration Quarterly, 43(2), 27-39.
- Paraskevas, A. (2001): Internal service encounters in hotels: an empirical study. International Journal of Contemporary Hospitality Management, 13 (6), 285-292.
- Paraskevas, A. (2003): Application Service Providers and Hospitality SMBs: High Promises - Low Response. International Journal of Hospitality Information Technology, 3(1): 61-73.
- Park, J.W., Robertson, R., & Wu, C.L. (2001): The effect of airline service quality on passengers behavioral intentions: A Korean case study, Journal of Air Transport Management, 10(6), 435–439.
- Parvatiyar, A. & Sheth, J.N. (2001); Customer Relationship Management: Emerging Practice, Process, and Discipline. Journal of Economic and Social Research 3(2), 1-34.
- Pathak, P. & Modi, P. (2004): Quality of Services: Issues and Challenges, An Indian Perspective. Synergy Journal of Management, 6 (1),75-80.
- Patton, M. Q. (2002). Qualitative evaluation and research methods (3rd ed.). Thousand Oaks, Sage Publications, Inc., UK
- Payne, A. & Frow, P. (2004): The Role of Multichannel Integration in Customer Relationship Management. Journal of Industrial Marketing Management, 33(6), 527–538.
- Payne, A. & Frow, P. (2005): A Strategic Framework for Customer Relationship Management. Journal of Marketing, 69(4), 167–176.
- Payne, A. (2006) Handbook of CRM, Achieving Excellence in Customer Management, Burlington, Butterworth-Heinemann, Oxford
- Payne, A. and Frow, P. (2010) Customer Relationship Management: from Strategy to Implementation, Journal of Marketing Management,

22, 135-168
- Pechlaner, H. & Raich, M. (2001): The Role of Information Technology in the Information Process for Cultural Products and Services in Tourism Destinations, Journal of Information Technology and Tourism, 4(2), 91-106.
- Pechlaner, H. & Tschurtschenthaler, P. (2003): Tourism Policy, Tourism Organisations and Change Management in Alpine Regions and Destinations: A European Perspective. Journal of Current Issues in Tourism, 6(6), 508-539.
- Peppard, J. (2000): Customer Relationship Management in Financial Services, European Management Journal, 18(3): 312–327.
- Peppers, D. & Rogers, M. (2004): Managing Customer Relationships: A Strategic Framework, 2nd Edition, Hoboken, NJ.
- Peppers, D. and Rogers, M. (1997), The One to One Future: Building Relationships One Customer at a Time,Currency/Doubleday, New York, NY
- Pérez, L.M., Polanco, R., Rios, J. C., Montealegre, J., Valderrama, L., Herrera, R., & Besoaín, X.(2007): The increase in endochitinases and β-1,3-glucanases in the mutant Th650-NG7 of the Trichoderma harzianum Th650, improves the biocontrol activity on Rhizoctonia solani infecting tomato. IOBC/WPRS Bulletin, 30(6), 135-138.
- Petrissans, A. (1999): Customer Relationship Management: The Changing Economics of Customer Relationship, Cap Gemini/ International Data, White Paper, May, p.95.
- Piccoli, G., O'Connor, P., Capaccioli, C. & Alvarez, R. (2003): Customer Relationship Management: A Driver for Change in the Structure of the U.S. Lodging Industry. Cornell Hotel and Restaurant Administration Quarterly, 44(4), 61 – 73.
- Piercy, N. (2002): Market-Led Strategic Change: A Guide to Transforming the Process of Going to Market (4th Edition), Butterworth-Heinemann, Oxford.
- Piskar, F. & Faganel, A. (2009): A successful CRM implementation project in a service company: case study. Journal of Management, Informatics & Human Resources, 42 (5), 199-208.
- Plakoyiannaki, E, & Tzokas, N, (2002): Customer Relationship Management: A Capabilities Portfolio Perspective. Journal of Database Marketing, 9(3), 228- 237.
- Plessis, M.D. & Boon, J. (2004): Knowledge management in e-business and customer relationship management: South African case study findings. International Journal of Knowledge Management, 24(1), 73-86.

- Po-An Hsieh, J.J., Rai, A., Petter, S. and Zhang, T. (2012) Impact of User Satisfaction with Mandated CRM Use on Employee Service Quality. MIS Quarterly. Vol. 36, Issue 4, pp.1065-1080.
- Puranik, R. (2013): A Study on Factors Influencing Customer Relationship Management of Telecom Companies. The Journal of Management, 4(3), 46-54.
- Raghunath S. & Joseph Shields (2001): Introduction of e-CRM in Indian Hotel Industry, CRM - Emerging concepts, Tata McGraw Hill
- Rahman, M., Hussain, T., Moon, S.P., Tisha, M.M., & Lima, M.T. (2021). Impact of Customer Relationship Management on Organizational Performance- A Study from the Perspectives of Bangladesh. Asian Business Consortium, 225-230.
- Rahimi, R., & Kozak, M. (2017): Impact of customer relationship management on customer satisfaction: The case of a budget hotel chain. Journal of Travel and Tourism Marketing, 34(1), 40–51.
- Raman, P. & Pashupati, K. (2004): Is CRM Really Doomed to Fail? An Exploratory Study of the Barriers to CRM Implementation, Journal of Customer Behavior, 3(1), 5-26.
- Raman, P., Wittmann, C. M & Rauseo, N.A. (2006): Leveraging CRM for Sales: The Role of Organizational Capabilities in Successful CRM Implementation. Journal of Personal Selling and Sales Management, 26(1):39-53.
- Ramana, V. Venkata, & Somayajulu, G. (2003): Customer Relationship Management - A Key to Corporate Success, Excel Books, New Delhi.
- Ramani, G. & Kumar, V. (2008): Interaction orientation and firm performance, Journal of Marketing, 72 (1), 27-45.
- Rameshwaran Byloppilly, (2021): An Empirical Study On The Influence of Customer Relationship Management On Customer Loyalty: A Special Reference To The Hotels In India, *SSRG International Journal of Economics and Management Studies*, 8(5), 107-119.
- Randolph W.A. & Dess G.G. (1984): The Congruence Perspective of Organization Design: A Conceptual Model and Multivariate Research Approach. AMR, **9 (1)**, 114–127, https://doi.org/10.5465/amr.1984.4278106.
- Rao, Rama (2005): Customer Relationship Management in India, Proceedings of the Seminar for Senior Executives of BHEL, Hyderabad.
- Reinartz, W.J., Krafft, M. & Hoyer, W.D. (2004): The customer relationship management process: its measurement and impact on performance, Journal of Marketing Research, 41 (3), 293-305.

- Richard, P. J., Devinney, T. M., Yip, G. S., & Johnson, G. (2009): Measuring organizational performance: towards methodological best practice. Journal of Management, 35(3), 718-804.
- Rigby, D.K. & Ledingham, D. (2004: CRM Done Right, Harvard Business.
- Riley, M., Niiininen, O., Szivas, E.E. & Willis, T. (2001): The Case for Process Approaches in Loyalty Research in Tourism. International Journal of Tourism Research, 3,23-32.
- Roberts, J. (2004): The modern firm: Organizational design for performance and growth. Oxford, Oxford University Press.
- Roberts, M. L., Liu, R. R. & Hazard, K. (2005): Strategy, technology, and organisational alignment: Key components of CRM success. Journal of Database Marketing & Customer Strategy Management, 12, 315-326.
- Rodríguez-Díaz, M. & Espino-Rodríguez, T.F. (2006): Developing Relational Capabilities in Hotels. International Journal of Contemporary Hospitality Management, 18 (1), 25-40.
- Rosman, R., & Stuhura, K. (2013): The Implications of Social Media on Customer Relationship Management and the Hospitality Industry. Journal of Management, 14(3), 19.
- Rūta Urbanskienė, Daiva Žostautienė, Virginija Chreptavičienė (2008). The Model of Creation of Customer Relationship Management (CRM) System. Engineering Economics, 3(58), 51-59.
- Ryals, L, and Payne, A. (2001) Customer Relationship Management in financial services: towards information-enabled relationship marketing, Journal of Strategic Marketing, Vol.9, No.1, pp.3-27.
- Ryals, L. (2005) Making Customer Relationship Management Work: The Measurement and Profitable Management of Customer Relationships. Journal of Marketing, 69, 252-261. https://doi.org/10.1509/jmkg.2005.69.4.252
- Ryals, L., and Knox, S. (2001) Cross-functional issues in the implementation of relationship marketing through CRM, European Management Journal, Vol.19, No.5, pp.534-542
- Ryals, L.J. & Knox, S. (2001): Cross-functional issues in the implementation of relationship marketing through customer relationship management. European Management Journal, 19 (5), 534-543.
- Ryals, L.J. & Payne, A. (2001): Customer relationship management in financial services: towards information-enabled relationship marketing. Journal of Strategic Marketing, 9(1), 3-27.
- Rygielski, C., Wang, J.C., Yen, D.C. (2002) Data mining techniques

- for customer relationship management. Technology in Society, Vol.24, pp.483-502.
- Sadek, H., Yousef, A., Ghoneim, A., Tantawi, P. (2011), Measuring the effect of customer relationship management (CRM) components on the non financial performance of commercial bank: Egypt case. European, Mediterranean and Middle Eastern Conference on Information Systems.EMCIS2011),May3031.Athens,Greece. Retrievedfrom.http://www.iseing.org/emcis/EMCISWe bsite/ EMCIS2011%20Proceedings/SCI10.pdf
- Sadri, G., & Lees, B. (2001): Developing corporate culture as a competitive advantage. The Journal of Management Development, 20 (10), 853- 859.
- Saha, Lewlisa, Hrudaya Kumar Tripathy, Soumya Ranjan Nayak, Akash Kumar Bhoi, and Paolo Barsocchi. (2021): Amalgamation of Customer Relationship Management and Data Analytics in Different Business Sectors—A Systematic Literature Review. Sustainability 13(9), 5279.
- Samppa Suoniemi., Harri Terho., Alex Zablah., Rami Olkkonen., & Detmar W.Straub (2021): The Impact of firm-level and project-level IT capabilities on CRM system quality and organizational productivity. Journal of Business Research, 127, 108-122.
- Sanjiv Kumar Srivastava, Bibhas Chandra & Gautam Shadilya (2018). Customer Relationship Management on Customer Loyalty and Retention in Hotel Industry in Jharkhand. International Journal of Civil Engineering and Technology, 9(1), 784-796.
- Santouridis, I & Tsachtani, E (2015): Investigating the Ompact of CRM Resources on CRM Processes : A Customer Life-Cycle Based Approch in The Case of Greek Bank, Procedia Economics and Finance Elsevier, 19, 304 – 313.
- Sathish, S., S.L. Pan & K.S. Raman (2002): Customer Relationship Management (CRM) Network: A New Approach to Studying CRM. Proceedings of Americas Conference on Information Systems, Association for Information Systems, Dallas, Texas USA, August 9–11.
- Scullin, S., Allotra, J., Lloyad, G. O. and Fjermestad, J. (2002) Electronic customer relationship management: benefits, consideration, pitfalls and trends, Proceedings of the IS one world Conference, Las Vegas, pp.1-14.
- Sekaran, U. & Bougie, R. (2010): Research Methods for Business: A Skill Building Approach, 5th ed., Wiley India, New Delhi.
- Shaheena Erkiah & Adjanu Damar Ladkoo (2018): A Quantitative

Study about Assessing the Effectiveness of Electronic Customer Relationship Management: A Case of Two Hotels in Mauritius. World Academy of Science, Engineering and Technology, International Journal of Science and Business Sciences, 12(10), 1439-1447.
- Shainesh G (2001) Customer Relationship Management. Mgmt Decision 6, 12-14.
- Shainesh, G. & Ramneesh Mohan (2007): Status of Customer Relationship Management in India, Management Development Institute Gurgaon, India.
- Shannahan, K.L., Shannahan, R.J., & Alexandrov, A. (2010): Strategic Orientation and Customer Relationship Management: A Contingency Framework of CRM Process. Journal of Comapative International Management, (1), 13.
- Shao, B.J, and Yu, T.K. (2004) The theory and practice of CRM, Tsinghua University Press©Chian.
- Sharp, Duane E. (2003): Customer Relationship Management Systems Handbook, CRC Press, Washington, USA.
- Shaw, G. & Williams, A. (2009): Knowledge transfer and management in tourism organization: An emerging research agenda. Tourism Management, 30(3), 325-335.
- Shaw, M.J., Subramaniam, C., Tan, G.W. and Welgb, M.E. (2001) Knowledge management and data mining for marketing. Decision Support Systems, Vol.31, Iss.1, pp.127-137.
- Shemwell, D.J., Yavas, U. & Bilgin, Z., (1998): Customer Service Provider Relationship: An empirical test of a model of service quality, satisfaction and relationship-oriented outcome. International Journal of Service Industry Management, (9)2, 155-168.
- Sherap Bhutia (2020): Sustainable Tourism for Regional Development in North-East States of India: Trends, Problems and Prospects. Global Journal of Human Social Science: B Geography, Geo-Sciences, Environmental Science & Disaster Management, 20(2), 20-34.
- Shi, J. & Yip, L. (2007): Driving innovation and improving employee capability: the effects of customer knowledge sharing on CRM. The Business Review, 7 (1), 107-112.
- Shikha Sota, Harish Chaudhry & Manish Kumar Srivastava (2019): Customer relationship management research in hospitality industry: a review and classification. Journal of Hospitality Marketing & Management, 29(1) 39-64.
- Shirazi, S. F. M., & Som, A. P. M. (2011): Destination management and relationship marketing: Two major factors to achieve competitive

- advantage. Journal of Relationship Marketing, 10(2), 76-87.
- Sigala, M. & Christou, E. (2002): Conceptualizing the measurement of service quality and TQM performance for hotels: The HOSTQUAL model. Journal of Acta Touristica. 14(2), 140-169.
- Sigala, M. (2003): Competing in the Virtual Market Space: A Strategic Model for Developing e-Commerce in the Hotel Industry. International Journal of Hospitality Information Technology 3 (1), 43-60.
- Sigala, M. (2003): Developing and Benchmarking Internet Marketing Strategies in the Hotel Sector in Greece, Journal of Hospitality and Tourism Research, 27(4), 375-401.
- Sigala, M. (2005). Integrating customer relationship management in hotel operations: Managerial and operational implications. Hospitality Management, Vol.24, No.3, pp, 391–413
- Sigala, M. (2005); Integrating customer relationship management in hotel operations: Managerial and operational implications. International Journal of Hospitality Management, 24, (3), 391-413.
- Sigala, M., Connolly, D. (2004): In search of the next big thing: IT issues and trends facing the hospitality industry – a review of the Sixth Annual Pan-European Hospitality Technology Exhibition and Conference (EURHOTEC 2001). Tourism Management, 25(6), 807-809.
- Sila, I. & Ebrahimpour, M. (2005): Critical linkages among TQM factors and business results. International Journal of Operations and Production Management, 25(11), 1123-1155.
- Sin, M. Tse, C.B., & Yim, H.K. (2005): CRM: conceptualization and scale development. European Journal of Marketing, 39 (11/12), 1264-1290.
- Sin, L.Y.M., Tse, A.C.B. & Chan, H. (2006): The Effect of Relationship Marketing Orientation on Business Performance in the Hotel Industry. Journal of Hospitality and Tourism Research, 30, (4), 407-426.
- Singh, Mohini (2002): The Role of e-mail Response in Customer Relationship Management. International Journal of Hospitality Management, 21(3), 428- 441.
- Sirirak, S., Islam, N. & Khang, B.D. (2011): Does ICT adoption enhance hotel performance?. Journal of Hospitality and Tourism Technology, 2 (1), 34-49.
- Soltani, Z., Zareie, B., Milani, F. S., & Navimipour, N. J. (2018): The impact of the customer relationship management on the organization performance. Journal of High Technology Management Research,

29(2), 237-246.
- Sotoudeh, Maryam (2007): Customer Relationship Management in the Tourism industry of Iran, Masters Thesis, Lulea University of Technology, Iran.
- Srinivasan, R. & Moorman, C. (2005): Strategic Firm Commitments and Rewards for Customer Relationship Management in Online Retailing. Journal of Marketing, 69(4), 193-200.
- Srivastava, S. & Kale, S.H. (2003): Philosophizing on the Elusiveness of Relationship Marketing Theory in Consumer Markets: A Case for Reassessing Ontological and Epistemological Assumptions. Australasian Marketing Journal, 11(3), 61-71.
- Stephen. P.B., Robin. S.K., & Mary. C (2002): Management. Pearson Education Ltd.
- Stone, M. & Foss, B. (2001) CRM in Financial Services, KOGAN PAGE.
- Strandvik, T. & Grönroos, C. (1994): Managing Customer Relationships for Profit: The Dynamics of Relationship Quality. International Journal of Services Industry Management, 5(5), 21-38
- Stringfellow, A., Winter, N. & Bowen, D. (2004): CRM: profiting from understanding customer needs. Business Horizons, 47 (5), 45-52.
- Subramanian, R. & Gopalakrishna, P. (2001): The Market Orientation-Performance Relationship in the Context of a Developing Economy: An Empirical Analysis. Journal of Business Research, 53(1),1-13.
- Sudhir, K.H. (2004): CRM Failure and the Seven Deadly Sins, Bond University's School of Business, Gold Coast, Swedish Institute, Sweden.
- Sultan Alshourah, Hamza Alassaf & Manal Altawalbeh (2018): Roles of Top Management and Customer Orientation in enhancing the performance of Customer Relationship Management (CRM) in Hotel Industry. International Journal of Advance Research and Innovation, 6(3), 233-239.
- Swar, B.N. (2012): Managing customers' perceptions and expectations of service delivery in selected banks in Odisha. The Indian Journal of Management, 5(2), 25-33.
- Swift, R (2001), Accelerating Customer Relationships Using CRM and Relationship Technologies, Prentice Hall PTR, UK.
- Swift, R.S. (2001): Accelerating Customer Relationships Using CRM and Relationship Technologies, Prentice-Hall, Englewood Cliffs, NJ.
- Tajeddini, K. (2010): Effect of customer orientation and entrepreneurial orientation on innovativeness: evidence from the

- hotel industry in Switzerland. Tourism Management, 31 (2), 221-231.
- Talón-Ballestero, P., González-Serrano, L., Soguero-Ruiz, C., Muñoz-Romero, S., & RojoÁlvarez, J. L. (2018): Using big data from Customer Relationship Management information systems to determine the client profile in the hotel sector. Tourism Management, 68, 187–197.
- Tanvi (2013): Studying the Comprehensive CRM Practices in Hospitality: A Critical Review. International Journal of Techno-Management, 01, (03), 1-13
- Tao, F.F. (2014) Customer Relationship Management based on Increasing Customer Satisfaction, Journal of Business and Social Science, Vol. 5, No. 5, pp.256-263.
- Thomas Chacko & Merlin Thanga Joy (2016): Customer Retention Strategies in Hotel Industry in Trivandrum. Journal of Chemical and Pharmaceuticals Sciences, 9(4), 1832-1836.
- Thursby, Jerry, G. (2000): What Do We Say about Ourselves and What Does It Mean? Yet Another Look at Economics Department Research. Journal of Economic Literature, 38 (2), 383-404.
- Tournois, L. (2004) Creating customer value: Bridging Theory and Practice, Marketing Management Journal, Vol.14, Issus, 2, pp.13-23.
- Trepper, C. (2000) "Match your CRM tool to your business mode". Information week. 15, 786
- Udunuwara, M. (2015): Customer relationship management (CRM) of hotels in the context of variety seeking behaviour (VSB). https://ro.ecu.edu.au/theses/1671.
- Van Tonder, E. & Roberts- Lombard, M. (2016): Customer loyalty guidelines for independent financial advisers in South Africa. Acta Commercii, 16, (1), 337. http://dx.doi.org/10.4102/ ac.v16i1.337.
- Vargo, S. L., & Lusch, R. (2004): Evolving to a new dominant logic for marketing. Journal of Marketing, 68(1), 1-17.
- Venkatesan, R. & Kumar, V. (2004): A Customer Lifetime Value Framework for Customer Selection and Resource Allocation Strategy. Journal of Marketing, 68(4),106-125.
- Verdugo, C.M., Oviedo-Garcia, A.M., Roldan, L.J. (2009): The employee-customer relationship quality: Antecedents and consequences in the hotel industry. International Journal of Contemporary Hospitality Management, 21(3), 251-274.
- Verhoef, P,C., Donkers, B. (2001) Predicting customer potential value an applicaiton in the insurance industry, Decision Support Systems, Vol.32, Iss.1, pp.189-199.
- Vicente Guerola-Navarro, Raul Oltra-Badenes, Hermenegildo Gil-Gomez & Jose Antonio Gil-Gomez (2020): Research model

for measuring the impact of customer relationship management (CRM) on performance indicators. Economic Research-Ekonomska Istraživanja, 34(1), 2669-2691. DOI: 10.1080/1331677X.2020.1836992.
- Vogt, C. (2011): Customer Relationship Management in Tourism: Management Needs and Research Applications. Journal of Travel Research, 50(4), 356-364.
- Wang, C., Huang, Y., Chen, C. & Lin, Y. (2010): The influence of customer relationship management process on management performance. International Journal of Organizational Innovation, 2(3), 40-51.
- **Web Sources**
- Webster, F.E. (2002) Marketing Management in Changing Times, Marketing Management, Vol.11, pp.1- 17.
- Werner Reinartz, Manfred Krafft, Wayne D.Hoyer (2004): The Customer Relationship Management Process: Its Measurement and Impact on Performance. Journal of Marketing Research, 41(3), 293-305.
- Wiklund, J., & Shepherd, D. (2003): Knowledge-based resources, entrepreneurial orientation, and the performance of small and medium-sized businesses. Strategic Management Journal, 24(13), 1307-1314.
- Wilson, A., Zeithaml, V.A., Bitner, M.J. & Gremler, D.D. (2012): Services Marketing, McGraw-Hill Education, UK.
- Wilson, H., Daniel, E. & McDonald, M. (2002): Factors for Success in Customer Relationship Management (CRM) Systems. Journal of Marketing Management, 18(1-2),193–219.
- Winer, R.S. (2001) A Framework for Customer Relationship Management, California management review, Vol.43, No.4, pp.89-105.
- Winer, R.S. (2001): A Framework for Customer Relationship Management. Journal of California Management Review, 43(4), 89–105.
- Wirtz, J.& Johnson, R. (2003): Singapore Airlines: what it takes to sustain service excellence - a senior management perspective, Managing Service Quality 13(1), 10-19.
- Woodcock, Neil et all. (2011): Social CRM as Business Strategy, Database Marketing & Customer Strategy Management, 18(1), 50-64.
- Woodruff, R.B. (1997) Customer Value: the next source for competitive advantage, Journal of the Academy of Marketing Science, Vol.25, Iss.2, No.139-153.

- Wu, S., & Li, P. (2011): The relationships between CRM, RQ and CLV based on different hotel preferences. International Journal of Hospitality Management, 30, 262-271.
- Wu, S., & Lu, C. (2012), The relationship between CRM, RM, and business performance: A study of the hotel industry in Taiwan. International Journal of Hospitality Management 31, 276–285.
- Wu, S.I. & Hung, J.M. (2007): The performance measurement of cause-related marketing by balance scorecard. Total Quality Management, 18 (7), 771-791.
- Wyner, G.A. (1999): Customer Relationship Management, Journal of Marketing Research, 11, 39–41.
- Xu, Y.R., Yen, C.D., Lin, B. and Chou, D.C. (2002) Adopting customer relationship management technology. Industrial management and data systems. Vol.8, No.102, pp.442-452.
- Yang, Z. (2005) Cooperate information management, Tsinghua University Press, China.
- Yen A., & Su L. (2004): Customer satisfaction measurement practice in Taiwan hotels. Hospitality Management, 23, 397–408.
- Yilmaz, C., Alpkan, L. & Ergun, E. (2005): Culture determinants of customer-and learning oriented value system and their joint effects on firm performance. Journal of Business Researches, 58 (10), 1340-1352.
- Yim, F.H.K., Anderson, R.E. & Swaminathan, S. (2005): Customer relationship management: its dimensions and effect on customer outcomes. Journal of Personal Selling and Sales Management, 24 (4), 263-278.
- Youssef Chetiovi & Hassan Abbar (2017): Customer Relationship Management (CRM) in Service Firms: A Model Proposal to measure the impact of the implementation of CRM dimensions on Hotel Performance. International Journal of Scientific and Engineering Research, 8(5), 289-307.
- Yuksel, A., Kilinc, U. K. & Yuksel, F. (2006): Cross-National Analysis of Hotel Customers' Attitudes toward Complaining and Their Complaining Behavior, Tourism Management, 27, (11-24). Zablah, A.R., Bellenger, D.N. and Johnston, W.J. (2004b), "An evaluation of divergent perspectives on customer relationship management: towards a common understanding of an emerging phenomenon", Industrial Marketing Management, 33 (6), 475-489.
- Zahay, D. & Griffin, A. (2004): Customer learning processes, strategy selection, and performance in business-to-business service firms. Decision Sciences, 35 (2),169-203.

- Zenab Soltani, Batool Zareie, Farnaz Sharifi Milani & Nima Jafari Navimipour (2018): The Impact of the Customer Relationship Management on the Organisational Performance. The Journal of High Technology Management Research, 29(2), 237-246.
- Zhou, K.Z., Brown, J.R. & Dev, C.S. (2009): Market orientation, competitive advantage, and performance: a demand-based perspective. Journal of Business Research, 62, 1063-1070.
- Zineldin, M. (1999): Exploring the common ground of total relationship management (TRM) and total quality management (TQM). Management Decision, 37(9), 719- 730.
- **Books**
- Handbook of CRM: Achieving Excellence in Customer Management, Adrian Payne, Butterworth-Heinemann, Elsevier, Oxford, London, 2005.
- **Websites:**
- https://hoteltechreport.com/news/hotel-crm
- https://smallbizcrm.com/crm-reading-lounge/crm-quotes-useful-quotations-about-crm/
- https://www.linkedin.com/pulse/future-hospitality-how-ai-powered-crm-revolutionizing-are-morch-a6ycc/#:~:text=The%20integration%20of%20AI%20into,in%20an%20increasingly%20digital%20marketplace.
- https://www.linkedin.com/in/aremorch?trk=article-ssr-frontend-pulse_publisher-author-card
- https://www.linkedin.com/pulse/what-scope-crm-hotel-industry-delmar-jos%C3%A9-ribeiro-s%C3%A1bio-ulzif/
- https://www.sunbasedata.com/blog/advantages-and-disadvantages-of-crm
- https://www.investindia.gov.in/sector/tourism-hospitality
- https://www.linkedin.com/pulse/importance-crm-tourism-industry-b-r3v/
- https://repository.dinus.ac.id/docs/ajar/Handbook_of_CRM.pdf
- https://hospitality.economictimes.indiatimes.com/news/speaking-heads/hospitality-trends-driven-by-ai-in-india/90903881
- https://www.cbre.com/insights/articles/ais-impact-on-hotels
- https://www.revinate.com/blog/everything-you-need-to-know-about-artificial-intelligence-in-hotel-technology/
- https://marutitech.com/hotel-industry-ai-awesome-user-experience/
- https://hospitality.economictimes.indiatimes.com/news/speaking-heads/the-impact-of-ai-driven-hotel-mapping-on-customer-

- satisfaction/110761276
- https://remora-solutions.com/concierge-robot/
- https://www.orangemantra.com/blog/7-industries-witnessing-impact-voice-technology/
- https://routemobile.b-cdn.net/wp-content/uploads/2021/11/03-CRM.png
- https://www.improvedapps.com/wp-content/uploads/2020/02/Improved-Apps-Realising-the-Benefits-of-CRM-White-Paper.pdf
- https://www.spinoffice-crm.com/blog/8-steps-to-developing-and-implementing-an-effective-crm-strategy/

Black Eagle Books

www.blackeaglebooks.org
info@blackeaglebooks.org

Black Eagle Books, an independent publisher, was founded as a nonprofit organization in April, 2019. It is our mission to connect and engage the Indian diaspora and the world at large with the best of works of world literature published on a collaborative platform, with special emphasis on foregrounding Contemporary Classics and New Writing.

www.ingramcontent.com/pod-product-compliance
Lightning Source LLC
Chambersburg PA
CBHW060610080526
44585CB00013B/769